# The
# Accidental
# Technology Trainer

## A Guide for Libraries

Stephanie Gerding

 Information Today, Inc.
Medford, New Jersey

*First printing, 2007*

*The Accidental Technology Trainer: A Guide for Libraries*

Copyright © 2007 by Stephanie Gerding

### Library of Congress Cataloging-in-Publication Data

Gerding, Stephanie
   The accidental technology trainer : a guide for libraries / Stephanie Gerding.
      p. cm.
   Includes bibliographical references and index.
   ISBN 978-1-57387-269-0
   1. Libraries and adult education.  2.  Information technology--Study and teaching.  3.  Library employees--In-service education.  4.  Training. 5.  Library surveys--United States.  I. Title.
   Z718.8.G47 2007
   025.5--dc22

160-2865                                                        2007035770

Printed and bound in the United States of America

President and CEO: Thomas H. Hogan, Sr.
Editor-in-Chief and Publisher: John B. Bryans
Managing Editor: Amy M. Reeve
Project Editor: Rachel Singer Gordon
VP Graphics and Production: M. Heide Dengler
Book Designer: Kara Mia Jalkowski
Cover Designer: Ashlee Caruolo
Copyeditor: Pat Hadley-Miller
Proofreader: Barbara Brynko
Indexer: Sharon Hughes

For my lovable husband, Patrick:
You are always the best part of my day.

# Contents

# Foreword

High on the list of subjects I wish I'd known more about when I started work was how to get other people to do new things. As the most recent hire and only person in my library who had ever tried database searching (this was a very long time ago!), I was made responsible for all technology-related reference activities. This work fell under "other duties as assigned," and the more experienced librarians seemed quite happy to let the new kid cope with the new tasks.

I, of course, wanted my colleagues to adopt the new technologies and incorporate them into their normal work routines. I tried asking them. I tried telling them. I even—with management's support—tried training them. But my notion of training was steeped in library traditions that venerate information and expertise. My approach went something like this:

1. Find a smart, authoritative person—an expert—who knows a lot about the topic.

2. Put that expert in a room with a bunch of comparatively ignorant (!) adults, the trainees.

3. Have the expert tell the trainees, in excruciating detail, what she knows, including what to do and how to do it.

4. The trainees will now understand the topic and change their behavior accordingly.

5. Or not.

The biggest problem with this approach is that it worked, sort of. Humans are a resilient species and can manage to learn under just about any circumstances. We did see modest improvements in the use of new technologies. It was also easy to document this kind of training on quarterly reports. Objective: Train at least 25 staff members in new search strategies. Check.

Even when this approach didn't work, we could always blame the trainees, who had, after all, been given all the necessary information. If they failed to modify their work habits, they apparently weren't well motivated, or feared change, or hadn't been paying proper attention. Their problem, not the trainer's.

Luckily for my long-suffering trainees, this "get the information right and all else will follow" approach can be pretty boring for the trainer after a while. If the content doesn't change, there's not much a trainer can do to keep things interesting for herself. So, for largely selfish reasons, I began to experiment with new techniques for delivering the material. The real breakthrough came when I realized that information is transferred much more readily when both the trainer and the trainees are interested and engaged in exploration.

I stopped trying to be an expert and started trying to be a facilitator. My job became supporting and encouraging other people's learning and discovery processes, while resisting my own deep-seated reference librarian's inclination to just tell them the right answers. It turned out that it was a lot more fun to provide training in this more collaborative way, and the experience was different every time. The training was much more effective as well. People started getting it, quickly and easily. Better yet, they started using what they learned, integrating the new skills and concepts seamlessly into their daily lives.

I wish I'd had this book to help me figure all that out when I was just getting started as a trainer. Stephanie Gerding's clear, well-organized, and supremely practical advice would have saved me time, trepidation, and a lot of embarrassing trial and error. Stephanie offers insights into training successfully in any kind of library setting, from formal courses to "teachable moments" at the desk or in the stacks. Step by step, with plenty of references, checklists, templates, examples, and insider tips from the library community's top trainers, her book will enable you to:

- Train others to use technology resources more effectively

- Communicate training information in a way that is clear, concise, and memorable

- Help your learners to become more self sufficient and self-motivating

- Deal effectively with "difficult" learners in a way that both serves them and keeps your own blood pressure down

It'll also make the training experience lots more enjoyable for you, the trainer—rookie or experienced, "accidental" or otherwise. Do yourself a favor and dive right in.

Joan Frye Williams
Library and Information Technology Consultant

# Acknowledgments

This book would not have been possible without the input of many fabulous library technology trainers. I thank everyone who took the time to complete a survey, share tips, or provide encouragement. I am proud to be part of a community that is so willing to contribute time and knowledge.

Thank you to my publisher, Information Today, Inc., for its support and educational opportunities for libraries, through print sources, online media, and conferences. Back in 2003, Information Today published my first professional article in *Computers in Libraries* magazine and has had a huge impact on my library career as an author and a trainer ever since.

Much gratitude goes to my outstanding editor, Rachel Singer Gordon. She works amazingly long hours, significantly contributes to and influences library literature and culture, and is an inspiration to many.

WebJunction—the organization, the Web site, the members, and *everyone* working there—has been very valuable to me, not only in writing this book, but as a trainer and librarian as well. Appreciation goes to the Bill & Melinda Gates Foundation for its support of WebJunction and libraries, and also for giving me one of the most amazing library training jobs of all.

Finally, I want to acknowledge some shining examples of what it means to be an excellent and dedicated library trainer, including Brenda Hough, Mary Bushing, Yolanda Cuesta, Sandra Nelson, Maureen Sullivan, and Mary Bucher Ross.

# About the Web Site

## stephaniegerding.com/accidentaltechtrainer

This book contains a number of useful Web sites and resources for accidental library technology trainers. An accompanying Web site has been created, which includes all of the links from this book and also new resources and articles of interest. To access it, go to stephaniegerding.com/accidentaltechtrainer. Please e-mail your comments or additions to the author at sgerding@stephanie gerding.com.

## Disclaimer

Neither the publisher nor the author makes any claim as to the results that may be obtained through the use of this Web site or of any of the Internet resources it references or links to. Neither publisher nor author will be held liable for any results, or lack thereof, obtained by the use of this page or any of its links; for any third-party changes; or for any hardware, software, or other problems that may occur as the result of using it. This Web site is subject to change or discontinuation without notice at the discretion of the publisher and author.

# Introduction

You are most likely reading this book because you are an accidental library technology trainer. Congratulations, and welcome to a large and growing group!

This book is for the many librarians who find themselves responsible for conducting technology training, whether in a computer lab, a classroom, or just one-on-one with the public. It provides reassurance by conveying practical methods for training success. Many new—and long-term  librarians are surprised to find that training is a large part of their jobs, despite the fact that they may not have been taught training skills in library school. Training may seem like a huge mystery, but with the help of this book, readers will be able to train more effectively, require less preparation time, and have successful training experiences in their libraries.

*The Accidental Technology Trainer: A Guide for Libraries* provides the tools and instruction you need, along with advice from library training experts with much wisdom to share. This book addresses the most common concerns I've heard from new trainers, including fear of failure, lack of confidence in front of groups, fear of public speaking, uncertainty about how to deal with difficult or unexpected situations, and worry about all the planning and details involved with training. If you are faced with technology training needs, are not sure what to do, or feel like you are flying by the seat of your pants, this book gives you the techniques, methods, and inspiration to go out and thrive as a trainer!

This book differs from general computer training manuals. It focuses on the library environment, which differs from corporate training settings in several ways. Most libraries, for example, do not charge for training, and library trainers must deal with a myriad of skill levels and an increased need for flexibility. Librarians, further, are often natural trainers, given their backgrounds in reference skills, information organization, programming (summer reading, reader's advisory), knowledge of resources, online searching and evaluation, information-seeking behaviors, and project planning.

Given the great variety in what libraries call the people they serve—patrons, customers, community members, clients—this book uses the terms "the public," "the learners," or just "the participants" to describe those on the receiving end of the training. I use the term "workshop" to describe any kind of organized training.

Much of the content in this book stems directly from my and other experienced trainers' personal experience in technology training in libraries around the country. In March 2007, I conducted an online survey and interviews with exemplary library technology trainers. I refer to these survey and interview responses throughout the book, and the trainers mentioned are listed in Appendix A.

The book progresses through what you need to know to be a successful accidental library technology trainer. Chapter 1, Being an Accidental Technology Trainer, answers basic questions, including: What is an accidental library technology trainer? How did this accident happen? Is it a happy accident? How do traditional library skills translate into training skills? Why should libraries provide technology training? What types of technology training do libraries usually offer?

Chapter 2, Discovering Training Principles, conveys basic training principles, including learning philosophies and theories, creating a learning community, and Learning 2.0. The chapter focuses on learning as an active process and the importance of learner-centered training. To be successful, a trainer should be more of a facilitator than a lecturer.

Chapter 3, Identifying Library Technology Training Skills, discusses the most important skills a successful technology trainer needs, and how to evaluate personal strengths and weaknesses in terms of these skills. These key training skills include: enthusiasm and attitude; social skills and building rapport; confidence in being yourself; subject knowledge; flexibility, patience, and empathy; respect; effective communication skills; facilitation and interaction; and planning skills. Readers will learn how to use their existing library skills and education within their new training responsibilities.

Chapter 4, Knowing Your Library Learners, stresses that learners vary based on interests, skill levels, age, attitudes, motivation, and learning styles. Only by knowing how different people learn can we plan and execute training most effectively. Common learning styles are explained, and advice is given on how to address learning preferences in training.

Chapter 5, Learning Interactively, shows the importance of using hands-on activities to ensure that learning not only happens but is retained. Interactive learning can be difficult for a new library trainer to understand, but it can transform how they train, increasing the odds of success for both the trainer and the participants. Examples of activities are included in this chapter.

Chapter 6, Creating and Maintaining Interest, works from the understanding that learning and retention cannot happen when a trainer loses participants' attention. The role of motivation and the importance of maintaining interest are often overlooked in training strategies, but they can be critical elements for success. Trainers need to make a workshop interesting, without making it purely entertaining. The reader will learn valuable methods for maintaining interest based on discussion of Abraham Maslow's hierarchy of human needs, David McClelland's theory of learned needs, and John Keller's ARCS motivation model.

Chapter 7, Planning Technology Training, demonstrates that, while trainers may be accidental, planning should always be purposeful. It is essential that trainers examine why technology training is needed at their library, so they can gain insight into the planning and resources necessary. This chapter also covers the importance of using the library's vision and strategic plan as the foundation for developing staff and public technology training plans. The common elements of a training plan are thoroughly examined, and examples are provided.

Chapter 8, Organizing and Designing the Workshop, takes planning to the micro level, discussing ways to plan individual workshops. Accidental technology trainers can become frustrated when they realize they have only 30 minutes of class time for an introductory Internet lesson that could take a week. By developing a workshop plan, trainers can organize their workshops, as well as share their planning with other co-workers. Readers will be encouraged with time-management techniques and learn how to: develop learning objectives; include short modules in their workshops; use training techniques; develop evaluation forms; create materials to share information; and focus on administrative details.

Chapter 9, Dealing with Difficult Library Training Situations, recognizes that accidental library trainers have to deal with a variety of difficult and challenging scenarios. Among these are: varied skill levels; challenging participants; technology failures; and registration problems. Readers will learn how to stay cool under pressure and how to deal with problems that can arise in workshops.

Chapter 10, Examining Best Practices in Library Technology Training, provides kernels of knowledge from interviews with library technology trainers from around the country. The chapter showcases their best practices, their most popular workshops, and their advice to accidental trainers. Special features include hot library workshops and examples of successful programs you can implement.

Chapter 11, Keeping Current and Sharing Resources, pulls together a wealth of information on where to find help, including blogs, lists, online and print resources, sources for curriculum and training ideas, and ways to share resources and recommended reading. An accidental library technology trainer may have fallen into the job, but his or her success from here on out depends on staying current and keeping classes from getting stagnant.

During a train-the-trainer workshop I once coordinated, a librarian pulled me into a stairwell to tell me how terrified she was of training, saying she just didn't think she could do it. Years later, this same librarian told me that she now conducts train-the-trainer workshops for other librarians, in which she tells them that she *used* to think training was the last thing she wanted to do, but now she loves it. She actively uses the interactive training strategies provided in this book to build confidence and skills in others. This is an outcome every trainer can look forward to, and the reason I have dedicated a good portion of my life to training.

I've done many different types of training throughout my library career for all types of libraries: school, public, academic, and special. I've presented at national conferences and conducted workshops across the U.S., from Seattle to Florida, Maine to California, and many places in between. I have trained thousands of librarians through my work with seven different organizations. Although I have had different titles and levels of responsibility, the one constant has always been the use of my training and technology skills. My training background includes:

- Automation training for Sirsi (now SirsiDynix)

- Computer use and maintenance training for the Bill & Melinda Gates Foundation

- Managing a statewide training program for all library staff at the New Mexico State Library

- Coordinating more than 200 continuing education programs yearly for the Arizona State Library, Archives and Public Records

- Teaching a distance learning course, Library Science 6010 Research Methods, for Northcentral University in Prescott Valley, Arizona

- Working as an independent library trainer and author conducting workshops across the U.S., primarily on the topics of training, library grants, emerging technologies, and strategic planning

Throughout these chapters, I have tried to provide tips, encouragement, and every bit of training knowledge I could squeeze out of my brain in the hope that you, too, can be empowered to go out and share your knowledge in the advancement of our libraries' goals. While writing, two questions were constantly on my mind: What does an accidental library technology trainer need to know? What will be most helpful to them? I hope to encourage and help other library technology trainers, as many have encouraged me. Accidental technology trainers will learn how they can leverage their natural skills and combine these with helpful new tips and tricks to be successful in their training.

Good luck and my best wishes!

Stephanie Gerding
sgerding@stephaniegerding.com

## Chapter 1

# Being an Accidental Technology Trainer

> *There is nothing training cannot do. Nothing is above its reach, it can turn bad morals to good; it can destroy bad principles and recreate good ones; it can lift men to angelship.*
>
> —Mark Twain

If you are like most library technology trainers, you were never taught how to train in school—or even when you began your first library position. So, you were probably surprised when you found out that your work responsibilities would include technology training, whether this meant formal classes in a computer lab or informal assistance while leaning over a patron's library monitor. You aren't alone.

## What Is an Accidental Technology Trainer?

Does being an accidental technology trainer mean that you teach classes in a computer lab? What if you teach online? Or create self-paced tutorials? Or just help someone set up an e-mail account? All of these activities constitute training. You might work in a public, school, academic, or special library. You might train library staff members, students, and/or the public. You could be a volunteer. You may have an MLS, or you might not. The common factor is simply that you didn't plan to do technology training in your library career.

If you have helped someone use Word, showed someone how to find a book in the online catalog, or shared tips on how to improve storytime, you've been a trainer. You helped someone learn. A trainer helps direct the growth of learners by helping them become competent or proficient in a skill or task. Trainers use coaching, instructing, and facilitating techniques to accomplish learning objectives.

A skillful trainer makes it easier for learners to learn by attempting to discover what a participant is interested in knowing, then determining the best way to make that information available by providing the appropriate knowledge, activities, or materials. This is done by listening, asking questions, providing ideas, suggesting alternatives, and identifying possible resources.

## How Did This Accident Happen?

When libraries need to select someone on staff to provide technology training, they naturally look to those with an interest in technology. Many accidental technology trainers fell into the role because they knew more about technology than their library co-workers, or even because they were the youngest staff members and thus assumed to be proficient in technology. In effect, these librarians were asked to take on the role of trainer simply because they were viewed as technology experts. Another group of accidental technology trainers fell into the role because they were enthusiastic about technology and wanted to share their knowledge and excitement with others. (This latter group might initially be more successful and happy with their accidental status!)

Successful technology training, though, has less to do with technical knowledge than with other abilities such as listening skills, patience, enthusiasm, and sympathy toward learners struggling with new technologies. Knowing how to train is more useful than just having technical expertise. I once sat on a panel of technology trainers who were giving a workshop for librarians. The three other panelists surely proved they knew what they were talking about, but the participants learned very little, because most didn't understand the terminology. Sometimes, keeping training simple and relevant is the most important thing you can do.

I became an accidental library technology trainer while working as an academic copy cataloger during library school. We started to use e-mail for the first time, and I was selected as Department E-mail Trainer. This first accidental technology training responsibility mainly involved one-on-one, just-in-time coaching. My first real training gig, however, was providing in-service training for a group of schoolteachers. Back in the mid-90s, I showed them the Internet for the first time—using the text-based Lynx browser! I am sure none of us realized then the real implications of what was to come.

My first professional library job was with the library automation company Sirsi (now SirsiDynix). The company's philosophy at the time (1997) was that it would rather hire someone who knew libraries and then teach them the technology, than hire someone who knew technology and then try to teach them about libraries. I thought that was rather brilliant. The library staff I trained appreciated examples that meant something to them and that I really understood their work and processes. By the time I began work for the Bill & Melinda Gates Foundation in 1999, I was no longer training accidentally, but this was the first time I received real instruction on being a trainer.

Curious about how the accident occurred for other library technology trainers? I interviewed some expert trainers and created an online survey to collect advice and details from a wide range of accidental library technology trainers. (A copy of the survey questions and information on the experts is included in Appendixes A and B.) It is quite inspiring to see how many library technology trainers got their start and their clear love of learning, technology, and sharing their knowledge and enthusiasm.

I asked trainers why they do technology training and received all kinds of answers:

- Someone asked me how to get an e-mail account.
- I'm young and enthusiastic.
- I was the most qualified.
- I was tagged "it."
- I just got my MLS, so they think I know technology.
- I knew how to turn the computer on.
- My boss made me.

## Survey Question: How Did You Become a Library Technology Trainer?

*Brenda Hough, Technology Coordinator, Northeast Kansas Library System, Lawrence (KS)* – "It was 1996, and I was a reference librarian at the Detroit Lakes Public Library, MN. We were newly automated and had just started offering public access to the Internet. I started out doing one-to-one training on the fly. We soon realized the need for more structured training and soon we were regularly offering classes for the public. It's been a part of my professional work ever since that time."

*Scott Hines, Reference Librarian, Pacific Graduate School of Psychology, Palo Alto (CA)* – "I became a technology trainer because I was doing technology work, but also loved teaching others about technology and helping others to use technology more effectively, and the need was great among faculty, staff, and other librarians."

*Meredith Farkas, Distance Learning Librarian, Norwich University, Northfield (VT)* – "It certainly wasn't my intention. I was interested in playing with technology and creating applications for the profession, but I never thought that I would be a very effective teacher. I started getting asked to give talks on the topics I knew a lot about, and I started to realize that I was good at teaching librarians about technology and that I really enjoyed it. I had always been uncomfortable with public speaking, so this realization was a big surprise to me."

*Anonymous* – "I pursued it. It is important to bring as many people as possible into the information loop."

*Max Anderson, Educational Services Librarian, SOLINET, Atlanta (GA)* – "While I was attending Florida State University's School of Information, I heard through another student about interviews for computer trainer positions at what was known then as the Gates Center for Technology Access (GCTA). I interviewed and was hired to be a Public Access Computer Trainer. Very soon after, the company merged with the Bill & Melinda Gates Foundation. I spent 3½ years traveling around the country installing computing technology in rural public libraries and training the staff how to use the technology, so they would know how to teach their patrons how to use the technology. I did not really know anything about technology before I started working with the Gates Foundation—everything I learned was through on-the-job training and internal training."

*Anonymous* – "I was an adult services librarian in a public library that decided to start offering basic computer instruction to the public. I was interested."

*Sarah Houghton-Jan, Information and Web Services Manager, San Mateo County Library, San Mateo (CA)* – "My first job out of library school was as an eServices Librarian for a county library system in California where part of my duties was to train on technology. Literally, the day I got there, I was told that they would be launching a timeout system on all of their public computers in three weeks, and that I needed to coordinate installation, integration, and staff and patron training in that time. So, let's say I became a technology trainer through a crash course from Hades. I had lots of previous training and teaching experience, so it wasn't a far stretch, but the technology training part of it was completely new to me before this position. Throughout my time there I learned how to best train on technology, and how it really is quite different than training on other topics. Now I train for my full-time job and as a consultant for InfoPeople, a nonprofit California group dedicated to training library staff throughout the state, mostly on technology."

*Anonymous* – "My position was created as part of an LSTA grant."

*Helene Blowers, Technology Director, Public Library of Charlotte & Mecklenburg County, Charlotte (NC)* – "I started as the library's first staff trainer back in 1996, right after the library began installing public access Internet PCs across the system. Prior to my arrival, staff did not have a technology resource on staff to assist them in gaining new skills that were required in the digital world."

*Bernadette Rivard, Supervisor of Technical Services, Milford Town Library, Milford (MA)* – "Our library's long range plan had a goal of offering technology training to the public. I applied for an LSTA Information Literacy Grant to meet that goal."

*Anonymous* – "I went to library school because it was moving into information technologies. I learned Web design, etc. while getting my MLS. Innovations and tools excite me so I want to share with others how they can be more efficient or have more fun!"

*Mindy Johnson, Head of Adult Services, Camden County Library, Voorhees (NJ)* – "I was hired as the 'Customer Education Librarian' in 2002, and the main part of my job was developing and teaching classes. Now, my position has changed, but I'm still teaching quite often."

*Anonymous* – "I became a technology trainer accidentally … a couple of my techier friends and I decided in January 2005 that we should give a brown bag that explained some common techie terms impacting libraries (cookies, proxy server, OpenURL, etc.). We called our presentation: 'What's a cookie, and why do I care if I can't eat it?' We got such a good turnout that we were asked to give it again and continued giving brown bags (approximately monthly) on PC or computer related topics."

*Susannah Violino, Reference Librarian, Norwalk Public Library, Norwalk (CT)* – "Reference librarians offer classes for the public."

*Erin James, Library Associate, Gwinnett County Public Library, Lilburn (GA)* – "By default and in self-defense! I help out at my branch only. I had previously worked as an administrative assistant, so my MS Office skills are relatively advanced. In the last few months, the system has moved to MS SharePoint—the people I work with are boggled, so I get to translate and train. Also, my bosses were so amazed that I had my own personal wiki for keeping track of staff development [that] I think they decided I must be an expert. Out of fairness, though, I should note that I was an English major and have absolutely no formal technology training. I love my computer and the Internet, so I've self-taught a lot over the years, and I enjoy finding answers to new questions."

*Mary Bucher Ross, training consultant, former manager of Staff Development, Seattle Public Library, Seattle (WA)* – "My path into training and staff development was such an amazing fluke. I was registered to attend a Washington Library Association conference on the Internet in 1996 (in the really early days of Web access in public libraries). One of the presenters got sick and had to cancel at the last minute, and the conference committee asked me and a coworker, Pat Grace, to take over his programs. At that time I had a few public Web access computers at the branch library where I was the manager and had done a number of classes on Web resources for teachers, seniors, community groups, etc. In the audience at the conference was

Susan Turner, director of continuing library education at the University of Washington (UW). She phoned me after the conference and asked me to teach a class for the UW Continuing Ed program for library practitioners. I ended up teaching four classes over a two-year period. Then, Seattle Public Library asked me to create a training program on Internet reference for its staff. That led to work with the Washington State Library and to my current involvement in staff training and development."

*Michael Porter, Community Associate, WebJunction, Seattle (WA)* – "Almost immediately in my first libary job in 1990 I was called on to informally train co-workers on basic computer use using our GEAC system. 'Accidental' really is the operative word here. 'Convenient' also comes to mind. It was really quite convenient for my library to use me for these training sessions. Having someone very comfortable with computers, who understood what buttons to push and why, was a less common skill set then than it has become today. The fact that I enjoyed helping folks get comfortable with the new technology was a happy convergence of these things; an accidental bit of convenient serendipity, you might say."

## Is It a Happy Accident?

Training has always been my favorite part of any job. It helps people, and it is exciting! As Robert Rosania wrote in *The Credible Trainer*, "One reason expressed countless times by many in the [training] profession is that training truly offers the potential to touch the hearts and minds of those people they serve."[1] This reminds me of librarianship. When I talk to people who work in libraries and ask them why they were initially attracted to the field, many say that it was because of their love of books and reading. But, when I ask them what they love most about their jobs, the most common responses mention the people they assist and their library's community. Though the inanimate book may have attracted them to library work, the people make the job rewarding and fulfilling.

Through training, you help people learn new skills, improve their performance with using a computer, and even show them new tools and fun social networking communities. This is a satisfying job, both professionally and personally. Technology trainer Michael Porter talks about the enjoyment training brings him:

> I taught my first "official" public technology class in 1996 (while working at the Allen County Public Library in Fort Wayne, Indiana). The ambitious title of that 90-minute long class was "Internet for Beginners." I remember being more excited about the content than nervous about teaching the class. This excitement has helped training stay fresh for me, more than a decade later. It's also an important point for folks that think they might want to pursue training as a large part of their career. Many years ago, when I complained about my job being boring or monotonous (pre-library, of course!), my grandma would say: "Well, that's why they call it work. They don't call it fun!" It's true that there are many "nose to the grindstone" tasks we need to accomplish. However, grandma also used to tell me that if I could find work that would allow me to get excited about going to the office in the morning, I would be doing pretty well. For me, when it comes to training and presentation, I get that excitement. I think it is important to recognize that, in order to be successful and happy with any work, some of our personal psychological needs must be met by that

work. It is satisfying psychologically to help, to be recognized by the student/learner community as a useful part of their existence. Not to put too fine a point on this issue, but this is a motivator both from the student and teacher perspective. It certainly is a huge part of why I still enjoy teaching, training, and presenting today. Seeing that flash of, "Oh yeah, this is cool, I can really use this!" across someone's face while you help them learn is a joyful experience that appeals to the psychology of both parties involved in the learning transaction. I can't imagine that ever just being "work," and these positive responses motivate me to strive to always improve the quality of my work and skills.

## How Do Traditional Library Skills Translate into Training Skills?

Accidental library technology trainers often discover that their existing library skills translate quite well to training. Many librarians seem to be natural trainers, as training has a lot to do with customer service and fulfilling the information needs of the participants. A background in reference skills, information organization, programming (including summer reading, reader's advisory, adult programming, or children's activities), knowledge of resources, online searching and evaluation, information-seeking behaviors, and/or project planning can be useful.

## Why Should Libraries Provide Technology Training?

We face the vital need to offer technology training in libraries; basic computer skills really matter. Many jobs, whether entry-level

## Transferable Skills

When asked how traditional library skills translate into training skills, the accidental technology trainers surveyed reinforced the idea that librarians are natural trainers. Comments included:

*Sarah Houghton-Jan, Information and Web Services Manager, San Mateo County Library, San Mateo (CA) –* "Patience, thoroughness, and organization are three stereotypical librarian skills that are quite useful for technology training as well. In fact, without them, you won't be much of a tech trainer at all."

*Anonymous –* "I conduct what are essentially reference interviews to determine the needs of my trainees, especially when doing 'Just in Time' or 'training on demand.' I naturally need to use my reference skills to gather good information and organizational skills to maintain training records."

*Scott Hines, Reference Librarian, Pacific Graduate School of Psychology, Palo Alto (CA) –* "I'd say that the primary skills from traditional library work that I use in technology training are reference interviewing and information literacy instruction. Information literacy instruction directly translates into technology training, of course, since it involves helping students to understand how they can use technology to get what they want and need. Reference interviewing is a particularly helpful skill in technology training because it helps tremendously in doing a quick needs assessment to find out exactly what the students need to know to accomplish their goals with technology."

*Colleen Eggett, Training Coordinator, Utah State Library, Salt Lake City (UT)* – "The traditional skills of how to research, how to find the information you are seeking, information literacy, the reference interview, and other topics I learned in library school remain the framework for what I teach."

*Anonymous* – "Most times, these tech tools are just tools to better a job or reach new users. For example, reaching more users can be done via MySpace, IM, podcasting, blogging, etc."

*Brenda Hough, Technology Coordinator, Northeast Kansas Library System, Lawrence (KS)* – "In each class, my goal is for each individual to gain something, to increase [his or her] conceptual understanding, or to resolve a question or area of confusion. I think it's somewhat like being a reference librarian and working with people as they do research. You assess where they are at and where they want to be, and then you help them move in that direction."

*Anonymous* – "The reference interview is always handy. What do people really want? Ask."

*Meredith Farkas, Distance Learning Librarian, Norwich University, Northfield (VT)* – "I think just about everything you do as a public services librarian involves instruction, though a lot of it is on a one-on-one basis. We're often teaching individual patrons how to do research in the databases, how to use the catalog, how to find something at the library, how to print, and much more. We're all about sharing information and helping people find the information they need. We are so used to sharing, that sharing what we know in a training situation comes quite naturally."

*Mary Bucher Ross, training consultant, Seattle (WA)* – "I was a children's librarian in a previous life, and that work was a wonderful preparation for training adults. The same principles of interaction that you use in storytimes work for adults who need to be involved in their own learning. If you can keep the attention of 15 three-year-olds for 30 minutes, you can be a trainer! Reference interview skills—open questioning techniques, non-verbal encouragers, clarification, and follow-up—are really skills for effective facilitation. If we truly believe that our role is to be facilitators of learning, rather than dispensers of wisdom, then we need to use open questions to promote reflective thinking … and not be afraid of silence."

*Chris Peters, Information Technology Specialist, Washington State Library, Olympia (WA)* – "Librarians are skilled at translating esoteric specialized knowledge into a general language that patrons understand. This is what trainers do as well. Patience and an ability to listen are crucial to both trainers and librarians."

or advanced, require some level of computer literacy. People of all socioeconomic backgrounds need to use e-mail, participate in Web-based training, or get online to apply for a job. Technology use isn't optional anymore; it's important in all areas of life. We can't ignore technology within the library, either. Library staff members all use computers and need the basic skills to support the day-to-day technology functions required by their jobs; technology impacts every library service we offer.

Technology has changed our expectations of what an educated person must know and be able to do in order to effectively participate in society. In 1983, *Time Magazine* named the computer "Man of the Year." In 2007, *Time*'s person of the year was YOU—due to the use of new social networking online tools. This evolution demonstrates a fundamental cultural shift. It is interesting to look back and read *Time*'s January 3, 1983, article, "The Computer Moves In," which talks about the new phenomenon of home computer use. Telecommuting is discussed and summarized as lacking the social interaction that humans crave. Companies that had tried letting employees work from home discovered that they "felt isolated, deprived of their social lives around the water cooler."[2]

Twenty-four years later, "*Time*'s Person of the Year: You" shows a dramatic shift in the use and view of technology:

> It's a story about community and collaboration on a scale never seen before. It's about the cosmic compendium of knowledge Wikipedia and the million-channel people's network YouTube and the online metropolis MySpace. It's about the many wresting power from the few and helping one another for nothing and how that will not only change the world, but also change the way the world changes. This is an opportunity to build a new kind of international understanding, not politician to politician, great man to great man, but citizen to citizen, person to person.[3]

More and more of our social interaction is moving online. We no longer just experience the digital divide; we now have to address technocultural isolation. Addressing this problem depends less on the technology and more on providing the skills and content that will be most beneficial. The Pew Internet & American Life Project (www.pewinternet.org) provides some useful statistics:

- 60 million Americans say that the Internet helped them make big decisions or negotiate their way through major episodes in their lives.

- More than half (55 percent) of all online American youths ages 12–17 use online social networking sites.

- Fully 87 percent of online users have at one time used the Internet to carry out research on a scientific topic or concept.

In 2006, the MacArthur Foundation launched a five-year, $50 million digital media and learning initiative to determine how digital technology is changing the way younger generations are learning, playing, socializing, and participating in civic life. The foundation is engaging in this substantial endeavor because it wants to inform social institutions, such as libraries, how we need to respond to the changing needs of our communities. One noteworthy paper it commissioned is *Confronting the Challenges of Participatory Culture: Media Education for the 21st Century*, which discusses cultural competencies and social skills as new media literacies that are developed through collaboration and networking in online community. Its author claims that a "participation gap" is occurring because some students don't have access to the new communities that are developing online. This results in not just a lack of technology for low-income children, but also a lack of opportunities for them to participate in society. "The new media literacies should be seen as social skills, as ways of interacting within a larger community, and not simply an individualized skill to be used for personal expression."[4]

The report states that "librarians … are reconceptualizing their role less as curators of bounded collection and more as information facilitators who can help users find what they need, online or off, and can cultivate good strategies for searching material." While some libraries strive to reach this goal, others don't even acknowledge this work as a library service priority. The report calls on after-school programs to be sites "of experimentation and innovation, a place where educators catch up with the changing culture and teach new subjects that expand children's understanding of the world. Museums, public libraries, churches, and social organizations can play important roles, each drawing on its core strengths to expand beyond what can be done during the official school day."

American Library Association (ALA) President Leslie Burger formed a task force in 2006 to create a National Library Agenda; the draft version was released in January 2007 (wikis.ala.org/national libraryagenda/images/f/f4/Discussion_Draft_MW_2007_final 1-11-07.pdf). The goal was to create a clear, compelling, and positive public message for all libraries, and to provide a focus for library activities. Library technology training addresses many of the six major theme areas in this agenda:

1. Libraries Preserve the Past and Provide a Bridge to the Future

2. Libraries Build and Strengthen Communities

3. Libraries Support Lifelong Learning

4. Libraries Create Information and Technology Literate Communities

5. Libraries Encourage Economic Development

6. Libraries Support Democracy

Library technology training, for both patrons and staff, plays a role in supporting all six areas. "Libraries Create Information and Technology Literate Communities," for instance, contains the

following description: "Technology offers unprecedented opportunities for critical thinking, information sharing, information
access and social networks. Great libraries offer opportunities for
all people to use new technologies and participate in the information society. Libraries in our communities, school and universities
should be a trusted destination for cutting edge technology that
provides for innovation, creation and connection."

And, in "Libraries Encourage Economic Development," we find:
"Our information-based economy requires a highly trained and
competitive workforce. Many people are unable to go back to
school to obtain the skills needed to participate in a 21st-century
workforce relying instead on libraries to supply the resources
needed to obtain new skills and work. At the same time the
increase in small businesses, home-based businesses and entrepreneurship finds many who relied on workplace libraries seeking
the assistance of local libraries when it comes to securing competitive intelligence, information about business start-ups, and business planning."

Libraries can help provide the skills and experiences needed to
become full participants in the social, cultural, economic, and
political future of our information-based society. Many groups
use online technologies to stay connected locally. People are con-
necting online in communities around reading, books, and information sharing. Much government information and commerce is
now only available online. Entrepreneurship through home-
based business, which tends to rely heavily on technology, is
becoming one of the most prevalent and permanent forms of
employment.

By offering the vital service of technology training to our communities, we can help create more satisfied customers, which, in turn,
are voters who are more supportive of libraries and their services.

## Survey Question: Why Should Libraries Provide Technology Training?

*Meredith Farkas, Distance Learning Librarian, Norwich University, Northfield (VT)* – "Libraries should provide technology training because it's a natural extension of what we already do. We already train patrons in how to use library resources, so teaching them how to effectively use other technologies makes perfect sense. In most public libraries, patrons are already coming to librarians for help with setting up e-mail, searching the Internet, and using other technologies. Offering training is just doing what we're already doing for individual patrons, but doing it for an entire group in an environment more conducive for learning. Training other librarians is crucial for providing good services to our patrons. If librarians are often looked to for help with technology, they need to be comfortable using these technologies. So often, public service librarians don't know how to fix printers, use scanners, and operate other basic equipment in the library. When called upon to deal with problems with these technologies, they are unable to help. In addition, librarians need to keep up with what technologies their patrons are using in order to see how these technologies might be applied in the library. Training can address both the basic library technology competencies that all public service librarians should have as well as teaching them about technologies that could be applied in libraries."

*Michael Stephens, Instructor, Graduate School of Library & Information Science at Dominican University, River Forest (IL)* – "One of the foremost roles of the library in the 21st century will be to guide users through the torrents of information available and teach them how to make sense of it. This role will also include instruction in how the systems work, or guided exploration. We're moving away from the step-by-step method of instruction. I would rather a trainer help users understand what resources are there, how to play with interfaces, and how to select the most appropriate information. We could say BI (Bibliographic Instruction) is dead, and librarian as information guide will be the wave of the future."

*Sarah Houghton-Jan, Information and Web Services Manager, San Mateo County Library, San Mateo (CA)* – "Libraries should provide as much technology training as possible to staff, and I mean staff at all levels, so that they can best serve our users—who at this point, let's be honest, know more about technology than the average librarian. Much of today's technology is focused on information retrieval and organization. To have library staff that are not proficient with those technologies is inexcusable. Look to Helene Blowers's well-known Learning 2.0 Program as an example of full staff integration into a tech training program. Libraries should provide increasing amounts of, and diverse types of, technology training to users because it's what they need to function in today's information economy. We have always served the information poor more than anyone else in our community, and today, that means serving the technology poor too."

*Max Anderson, Educational Services Librarian, SOLINET, Atlanta (GA)* – "I think the most important reason for why libraries should provide technology training is that patrons expect and want it. It not only empowers patrons in their

> abilities with technology for the future, it also allows the library staff to keep up-to-date on technology and practice their training skills. It's a win-win situation."

## What Types of Technology Training Do Libraries Usually Offer?

I've conducted technology training workshops in rural and urban areas across the U. S. and am always amazed that the same basic training skills are still needed, especially in rural libraries. (The answers to the online survey reflect this need as well.) Chapter 10 includes many innovative ways that libraries are doing technology training beyond these basics, such as training on emerging technologies. The most common workshops, however, are offered on:

- Internet (introductory and intermediate)
- Computer basics, such as using the mouse and organizing files
- Microsoft Applications such as Word, Excel, PowerPoint, and Publisher
- E-mail and e-mail culture
- Web design
- Database and catalog searching

## Is Technology Training Different Than Other Kinds of Training?

Training on technology topics definitely evokes different issues than training on soft skills. First, you do have to have some technical

### Survey Question: What Types of Technology Workshops Are Offered by Your Library?

*Helene Blowers, Technology Director, Public Library of Charlotte & Mecklenburg County, Charlotte (NC)* – "For staff, we offer training in four areas: technology, electronic resources, library skills (such as reader's advisory and the reference interview), and management and supervisory skills. For patrons, our technology workshops cover the spectrum, from basic mouse skills to exploring new and emerging technologies such as Web 2.0 tools (Flickr, Picasa, MySpace for Parents, etc.)."

*Anonymous* – "Each branch library offers a variety of basic programs: basic Internet classes, how-to-use e-mail, Web browsing, digital photography. We haven't delved into advanced topics yet. Currently, the most basic classes (basic Internet and e-mail) are still the most popular classes that our libraries offer."

*Bernadette Rivard, Supervisor of Technical Services, Milford Town Library, Milford (MA)* – There are five classes in the Information Literacy Series: Using the Online Catalog; Finding and Evaluating Information on the Internet & in the Library Databases; Researching Medical Conditions & Prescription Drugs; Researching Jobs, Careers & Companies; and Researching Purchasing a Consumer Product. There are also five classes in the Microsoft Office Series: Word, Excel, PowerPoint, Publisher, and Access."

*Scott Hines, Reference Librarian, Pacific Graduate School of Psychology, Palo Alto (CA)* – "We offer technology workshops in EndNote bibliographic instruction software and also on how to use Adobe Acrobat Professional, and informal training on MS Word, Excel, and PowerPoint, but in my previous job, I did formal classes on Windows, Word, Access, Excel, ColdFusion, PHP, XML, using the network, Web design, open source software, using e-mail, using and administering Blackboard and WebCT, and working with experts on technology projects."

expertise. And we all know that using technology can cause certain problems in and of itself, such as unreliability. You can't do technology training just anywhere, you do need to have some kind of equipment—preferably a hands-on environment like a computer lab. Then, you also have to maintain and update that equipment.

But are the skills needed to do technology training different than those we use to train on other topics? Learning is about change. It doesn't really matter if training is about soft skills or technological topics; the fundamental principles are the same. In their book *Telling Ain't Training*, authors Stolovitch and Keeps assert: "To summarize hundreds of studies, the effectiveness of messages aimed at learning is not bound up in the delivery vehicle but rather in how the message itself is designed ... Self-paced print or sophisticated, electronically delivered instruction is only as effective as the instruction design principles that are applied."[5]

Chapter 2 examines some universal training principles, the most important of which is to have the participants actively involved in the learning process.

## Endnotes

1. Robert Rosania, *The Credible Trainer*, Alexandria, VA: ASTD, 2001: 2.

2. Otto Friedrich, "The Computer Moves In," *Time Magazine*, Jan. 3, 1983. Accessed March 29, 2007 (www.time.com/time/printout/0,8816, 953632,00.html).

3. Lev Grossman, "Time's Person of the Year: You," *Time Magazine*, Dec. 13, 2006. Accessed March 29, 2007 (www.time.com/time/magazine/ article/0,9171,1569514,00.html).

4. Henry Jenkins, "Confronting the Challenges of Participatory Culture: Media Education for the 21st Century," The MacArthur Foundation. Accessed March 29, 2007 (www.digitallearning.macfound.org/site/c.en JLKQNlFiG/b.2029291/k.97E5/Occasional_Papers.htm).

5. Harold Stolovitch and Erica Keeps, *Telling Ain't Training*, Alexandria, VA: ASTD, 2002: 14–15.

## Chapter 2

# Discovering Training Principles

*If in an educational situation an adult's experi-
ence is ignored, not valued, not made use of, it is
not just the experience that is being rejected, it is
the person.*

—Malcolm Knowles

Training is an art more than it is a science. There is no one right
way to conduct training, and no two workshops are ever exactly
the same; quite a bit of creativity goes into good, active training. I
didn't know educational or learning theory when I began working
as a library technology trainer. I didn't have real train-the-trainer
instruction until my third job. But understanding the basics of how
participants learn and what we can do as trainers to assist with this
process can be extremely helpful for any accidental library technology trainer.

Learning is the act by which a change occurs in a person's
behavior, knowledge, skills, and/or attitudes. So really, learning is
about change in a person, and training is how we help bring about
that change. In psychology and education, learning theories
describe how people learn and help explain the inherently complex process of learning. There are many of these theories and as
many perspectives on those theories.

Most of these theories aren't exactly revolutionary, though there
always seem to be new variations and models. Look back to
ancient teaching methods and the ways in which learning was perceived to be a process of mental inquiry, and see how we still use

similar techniques today. For example, the Chinese used what we now call case studies, in which the trainer describes a sample situation and the participants explore resolutions. Then, there is the Socratic Method, in which the trainer poses a question or problem and the participants respond with an answer or solution.

Current training models use the terms learner-centered instruction, active participation, accelerated learning, and even Learning 2.0. These are connected by the common principles that training is a process in which the content must be determined by the participants' needs, the methods need to be geared toward individual abilities, and the design must involve active participation.

These models are the opposite of a traditional lecture style. As is often said, the trainer has to learn to be the "guide on the side, not the sage on the stage." We need to teach people how to learn, not just give them step-by-step instructions that will work only in one software program or only for one task. As Paul Clothier writes in *The Complete Computer Trainer*: "Imagine a computer class where the learners are relaxed; find the information stimulating, easy to follow, and remember; learn more; and have fun. It might sound a little utopian for some seasoned trainers, but I assure you, it is possible."[1] Training is a process, not an event.

## Andragogy

Malcolm Knowles transformed the field of adult training, particularly in regard to informal, nonacademic education. He explored the idea of andragogy, a learning theory for adults, as distinct from pedagogy for children. Andragogy refers to a set of six core adult learning principles that involve a learner-centered approach, as opposed to a content-centered approach: 1) the learner's need to know; 2) self-concept of the learner; 3) prior experiences of the learner; 4) readiness to learn; 5) orientation to learning; and 6) motivation to learn.

Andragogy places importance on process design over content design. A trainer focused on process design will include learning experiences and involve the participant throughout the entire training. As Malcolm Knowles, et al. explains in *The Adult Learner*: "The difference is not that one deals with content and the other does not; the difference is that the content model is concerned with transmitting information and skills, whereas the process model is concerned with providing procedures and resources for helping learners acquire information and skills."[2] This means that a trainer using an andragogical approach will focus on building a mutually respectful, collaborative, experiential workshop that will involve the participant in self-directed, proactive learning.

In his 1950 book, *Informal Adult Education*, Knowles laid out the challenge that adult learning should be a laboratory of democracy.[3] He outlined outcomes for adult learners, some of which may seem very lofty, but all of which are admirable goals. Table 2.1 lists these outcomes and tips on how trainers can achieve them.

Table 2.1  Adult Learner Outcomes and Strategies

| Knowles' Adult Learner Outcomes | Trainer Strategies to Achieve the Outcomes |
|---|---|
| "Adults should acquire a mature understanding of themselves." | You can help participants to identify and understand their own needs, motivations, interests, capacities, and goals. |
| "Adults should develop a dynamic attitude toward life." | You can address the positive aspects of change, and demonstrate how any experience is an opportunity to learn. |
| "Adults should learn to react to the causes, not the symptoms, of behavior." | You can focus participants on the root of problems. |
| "Adults should acquire the skills necessary to achieve the potentials of their personalities." | You can encourage participants to achieve their highest capacity of learning. |
| "Adults should develop an attitude of acceptance, love, and respect toward others." | You can incorporate the importance of learning to challenge ideas but not people. |
| "Adults should understand the essential values in the capital of human experience." | You can encourage and acknowledge each participant's experience and give him or her opportunities to share their knowledge with each other. |
| "Adults should understand their society and should be skillful in directing social change." | You can incorporate democratic decision making—making intelligent decisions for the entire population, and encouraging acceptance of individual differences. |

## Constructivist Learning

Constructivist Learning Theory postulates learning as an active process of creating meaning from experiences. In other words, people learn best by trying to make sense of something on their own, with the teacher as a guide to help them along the way. Learners have a view of what the world is like and how it operates; they adapt and transform their understanding of new experiences in light of their existing knowledge. Trainers must recognize how a learner already sees the world, and how that learner believes it to operate. New information presented to the learner will be modified by what she or he already knows and believes.

Constructivism views learning as a process in which the learner actively constructs, or builds, new ideas or concepts based on both current and past knowledge. This is a very personal endeavor, with the aim that what is learned in a workshop may be applied in a practical, real-world context. The trainer acts as a facilitator who encourages participants to discover for themselves and to construct knowledge by working to solve realistic problems. Constructivism promotes free exploration. Trainers adjust their workshops based on participants' input, encouraging them to analyze, interpret, and predict information. Trainers also rely heavily on open-ended questions and promote extensive dialogue among participants.

When a learner can assimilate information and can find a relationship by which the information can be associated with their existing knowledge, learning becomes easier. In constructivism, understanding prior learning and each person's background and knowledge becomes very important. This also makes it important to present information from different perspectives as well as with different sensory modes.

Expert trainer Mary Bucher Ross states: "I am firmly in the constructivist camp when it comes to training design." Her explanation of this approach was written for Seattle Public Library trainers involved with a virtual reference training program (vrstrain.spl. org/vrstrainer.htm):

> This training curriculum is based on a constructivist approach to distance learning. Some characteristics of constructivism:
> - Stresses collaboration over individual learning
>
> - Is more learner-focused, less teacher-focused
>
> - Is contextual, builds on previous learner experiences
>
> - Emphasizes exploration, discovery, and reflection
>
> As a trainer, your most important roles will be to:
> - Support and encourage the learners, providing extra assistance whenever needed
>
> - Facilitate an active, collaborative learning environment
>
> - Provide positive feedback on each learner's contributions
>
> - Ask the right question rather than give the right answer

## Creating a Learning Community

A learning community in a technology workshop starts with a feeling of safety and comfort. Help participants connect with each other, with the topic, and with you. In *The Ten-Minute Trainer*, Sharon L. Bowman explains that: "By encouraging learners to interact, appreciate each other, and learn from each other, you're creating a learning community that is a group of people who interact in positive ways and who are emotionally invested in helping each other learn."[4]

One simple method I use to help create a comfortable atmosphere is to begin a workshop with four "rules." I tell participants they must: 1) make mistakes, 2) ask stupid questions, 3) cheat, and 4) have fun. I explain that our workshop is going to involve hands-on work, and that it is better for them to make mistakes now than when they go home. I remind them that they really won't break the computer. I tell them I encourage stupid questions, because usually someone else is wondering the same thing. I will pause during the workshop and ask if anyone has a stupid question for me. This usually brings about a few laughs at some point, when someone raises their hand, says they have a stupid question, and I thank them for following my rules. The cheating rule breaks their association with traditional school classroom restrictions. I tell them they can look at each other's computer screens, learn together, and ask each other for the answers. Of course, having fun is part of active learning as well.

Accelerated learning (AL) addresses the collaborative learning community. AL combines adult learning theory and whole brain learning theory to achieve a faster learning rate. Learners learn content as well as critical thinking, communication, and social skills. Dave Meier's *Accelerated Learning Handbook* gives seven indicators to describe this type of learning:[5]

1. A community collaborating vs. a collection (classroom) of individuals.

2. Learning involves the whole mind and body.

3. Learning is creation not consumption.

4. Learning engages us on many levels.

5. Learning comes from doing the work itself.

6. Positive emotions improve learning.

7. Images are easier to grasp than verbal abstractions. Use visuals to drive home the point.

Learners need to have a role in the planning of the training. This may sound difficult, but it can be done. Trainers need to develop their skills as facilitators and aim to be learning guides; adults need to be self-directed. Participants will be more committed to the training if they help influence the topics. You can give them a list of six objectives, for instance, and have them pick the four they are most interested in focusing on. See Figure 2.1 for an Unshelved comic strip that presents an extreme example of how a librarian could use this method.

The workshop you design is like the framework of a house being built, just the bare skeleton of beams and structure. The participant then adds the drywall, the roof, the windows, and the doors. Advanced learners might be working on the inside decor. You give them the structure, but they incorporate their own details based on their knowledge and their own needs. Try to find ways to connect with what each individual finds personally meaningful.

This concept is explained in *The Adult Learner:* "When learners understand how the acquisition of certain knowledge or skills will add to their ability to perform better in life, they enter into even didactic instruction situations with a clearer sense of purpose and see what they learn as more personal."[6]

One technique that helps is what I call organized flexibility, in which you just have to learn to go with the flow and not be tied to an exact agenda. I recently gave an all-day workshop. It was after lunch (which had been pasta!), the room was getting really warm, and the participants' eyes all glazed over at once. I knew that I could keep going with my plan, but that no learning would actually take place under those circumstances. So I stopped the workshop, the participants got up and stretched, we opened the windows, and then they were ready to learn again. We lost 10 minutes of workshop time, but we regained attention and focus.

## Learning 2.0

Originally referred to as eLearning 2.0, Learning 2.0 is an instructional philosophy that emphasizes a flexible, hands-on,

Figure 2.1   Unshelved Comic Strip, Jan. 22, 2006. (Copyright Overdue
Media, LLC, www.overduemedia.com. Used with permission.)

and often informal learning environment. Usually centered on learning about Web 2.0 technologies, Learning 2.0 encourages paricipants to learn on their own and explore new social communitites and online collaboration. The role of the participant is as a creator and a contributor.

Learning 2.0 emphasizes that everyone has a critical role to play in contributing to the overall learning experience. The participant creates and discovers what is to be learned through personal experiences in his or her own learning environment. The participant is also responsible for selecting the technologies he or she needs to learn about, asking for assistance, or finding his or her own sources of information outside of the provided environment and bringing that knowledge back to the group.

The role of the trainer is as faciliator, environmental provider, and content/conversational shepherd. The trainer is not to act as the expert, or even, in some cases, as the designer of the learning experience itself. Rather, the trainer is a facilitator who provides and/or structures the environment in which the learning occurs. This may involve the initial introduction of learning elements into the environment and playing a "quality assurance" role as participants progress through the learning program. Helene Blowers of the Public Library of Charlotte & Mecklenburg County introduced a Learning 2.0 program for staff in August 2006. You can read more details about this program in Chapter 10.

## Endnotes

1. Paul Clothier, *The Complete Computer Trainer*, New York: McGraw-Hill, 1996: 252.
2. Malcolm Shepherd Knowles, Elwood F. Holton, and Richard A. Swanson, *The Adult Learner: The Definitive Classic in Adult Education and Human Resource Development*, Amsterdam: Elsevier, 2005: 115.
3. Malcolm Shepherd Knowles, *Informal Adult Education: A Guide for Administrators, Leaders, and Teachers*, New York: Association Press, 1950: 9–10.

4. Sharon L. Bowman, *The Ten-Minute Trainer: 150 Ways to Teach It Quick and Make It Stick!* San Francisco: Pfeiffer, 2005: 152.
5. Dave Meier, *The Accelerated Learning Handbook: A Creative Guide to Designing and Delivering Faster, More Effective Training Programs*, New York: McGraw Hill, 2000: 9–10.
6. Knowles, *The Adult Learner,* 125.

## Chapter 3

# Identifying Library Technology Training Skills

*Give the pupils something to do,*
*Not something to learn;*
*And the doing is of such a nature*
*As to demand thinking;*
*Learning naturally results.*

—John Dewey

What skills do you need to be a great technology trainer? You might be surprised to learn that the most important skill for a successful technology trainer is *not* technological expertise! Success in technology training depends on the same fundamentals as any kind of quality training, many of which stem from a trainer's own character and social skills. These involve the ability to create a safe, active learning environment and the capacity to be organized, creative, and focused on ways to help others learn.

This chapter explores the most important skills and abilities for a successful library technology trainer, and talks about ways to evaluate your personal strengths and weaknesses. You acquire the most important training skills through work experience, life experience, study, and training. These include enthusiasm and attitude; social skills; self-confidence; subject knowledge; empathy, patience, and flexibility; respect; communication skills; facilitation and interaction; and planning skills. Remember: Training is all about helping people learn, which librarians often do already as part of their other services.

## Enthusiasm and Attitude

A great trainer has passion—passion for learning and passion for passing it on. Great trainers are interested in people; they are engaged and able to get and keep their participants engaged. They are interested in how people learn and in building participants' self-confidence.

You don't have to be a completely polished presenter, and you don't have to memorize your training word-for-word. This isn't theater, and there shouldn't be a script. To be learner-centered, find ways to enjoy what you are doing, share this enthusiasm, and put the people first. It isn't what the trainer *says* that influences the amount of learning; it is how learners are helped to create their own knowledge. Your most important goal is to involve participants, getting them to talk, think, share, and act.

It can be difficult to maintain enthusiasm after teaching "Introduction to the Internet" for the 31st time. But try to find a way to make training more exciting for you. Use a new exercise, bring in a guest trainer, use a different fun review activity, or incorporate a topical or decorative theme; somehow make the workshop different. This will keep it fresh for you—and also for the participants, who will otherwise pick up on your boredom.

You should never let participants think that you don't want to be there, which just encourages them to think the same way. Never tell them that you were tricked into teaching the workshop, that your boss is making you do this, or flippantly comment that "*they* think I know something about this, so *they* are making me teach this"—even if it is true. Demonstrate that you are credible and let participants know what you enjoy about the topic. (There must be something, even a personal reason.) Share with them how you use the technology in your professional and/or personal life.

Just as you shouldn't be a downer for the participants, give yourself the same respect and avoid negative self-talk. Don't go into a workshop thinking: *This is going to be the worst workshop I've ever done,* or *I don't know why I agreed to do this. What was I thinking?* or *What if I don't know enough? Why didn't I practice more? Why didn't I create a handout for this workshop?* Don't do it. Just don't go there. It really won't be helpful and can actually make you less capable. Instead, reassure yourself, even if you feel a little silly about it. Tell yourself: *This is going to be a great class. I'm excited to be here. I can't wait to meet these participants and help them learn.* It may sound goofy, but it really makes a difference.

Make your classes fun, but remember that you can't fake humor. If you aren't a funny person, just try to have fun in the class yourself. Remove the boredom. Start off the workshop by saying that you want to have fun. This lets people know it is OK to laugh and even for them to joke a little. Participants appreciate most attempts at humor and fun. Laughing does help learning!

You can also add a simple fun exercise to help energize both you and the participants, while also helping reinforce the material they are learning. Examples of activities are provided and discussed in Chapter 5.

## Social Skills

You've probably heard stories and read articles about first impressions, how they are made in the first minute and how interviewers decide whether they are going to hire you in the first three minutes. Talk about pressure!

The beginning of a workshop is equally important. Try to personally greet each person as they come into the training room. If you can make a connection, even better, but at least introduce yourself and try to make them feel more comfortable by removing the barriers that traditionally exist between teachers and students.

Act like you are welcoming participants to your house. Some trainers don't talk to people before the workshop begins. They shuffle papers, fiddle with their PowerPoint, or hide out in the back of the room. You don't do this when you invite people over to your home. You welcome them as they come in the door and introduce yourself. You ask them how they are doing, how the drive was, or make other small talk.

Do the same thing with your workshop participants. For them, the workshop begins when they walk in the door, not at 9 AM when you stand up and say "Good morning." If they enter feeling unwelcome and unsure of what is going on, they will have a learning block from the beginning. Help them feel comfortable. And the great thing is that this will help you feel comfortable as well! Learn something about them, break the trainer/participant barrier, and start the workshop with participants who are new acquaintances rather than strangers.

You need to be comfortable with people to be a good trainer. Public services staff are sometimes better with people than technical services staff, although this isn't always the case. Someone used to answering reference questions and dealing with random situations that happen in the library can be more suited to training than someone who prefers to stay in the back room on the computer. Social skills are an important part of a great trainer's toolbox.

Participants need to continue feeling comfortable and safe throughout the workshop. Just remember that, if they are uncomfortable, they won't learn. Here's an example: I once attended a workshop with about 70 other people. We had flown a trainer in from out of state to do a technology workshop. At the beginning, she asked the participants to raise their hand's if they did *not* know what a blog was. No hands were raised. She said: "OK, good," and went on to talk about blogs without a definition or explanation. I was surprised that so many of these librarians knew about blogs. At the first break, I asked someone if they knew what a blog was. They said "No, but I wasn't going to be the only one to raise my hand!" I asked several others, and they admitted they didn't know either. They were uncomfortable admitting ignorance in front of their peers.

I use this example when conducting an introductory emerging technology workshop. I tell participants what happened, then tell them that, in this workshop, we are going to learn together, and that we are safe here to admit anything we don't know. I tell them that I don't know it all and I'm still learning. Then I ask them to raise their hands if they don't know what a blog is. They usually laugh and quite a few raise their hands. From that point on, they feel safe admitting when they don't know something.

In that original workshop, if the question had been asked another way, the entire outcome would have been different. Everyone at that workshop who didn't know what a blog was felt foolish, like they were the *only* one who didn't. So, they quietly sat there, even though they didn't have a clue what the trainer was talking about. The trainer really did want to know what people knew and would have explained blogs. She just needed to make sure they felt comfortable telling her. Even adjusting the question to ask it this way, "Many of you probably don't know what a blog is—raise your hands if this is true," lets participants know ahead of time that they won't be the only ones raising their hands, and that not knowing isn't uncommon or shameful.

Another important part of building rapport is honesty. You must have people's trust. You gain more credibility by acknowledging that you don't know an answer than by giving a wrong answer or trying to fake it. Maintain your credibility by being honest and sincere.

## Self-Confidence

Be yourself—don't fake it. Use your own training style and always remember that a smile is powerful. I've seen too many trainers display an entirely different persona when in front of a group. They get in front of a classroom and start to grip the podium, use difficult words and terminology, and try to portray an image of expert knowledge. This is not conducive to learning! It just bores people, who will tune out and start making grocery lists on the back of their handouts. Learning comes to a halt. Formality is *not* necessary for learning. Technology trainer Michael Porter wrote in his survey answers: "I try to play to my personal strengths. Humor works for me. Well, most of the time. If nothing else, I can poke fun at myself for cracking a joke nobody thought was funny!" Try to figure out what your own strengths are and use them in your training.

It's important and comforting to realize that your participants want you to succeed. Learners don't want to sit through a boring, uncomfortable workshop, watching a nervous speaker. They want a supportive trainer, and they want to have a good time learning.

Practice is the key to becoming more comfortable. In library school, I set a personal goal to become a better speaker. As I was most nervous when speaking in front of my peers, other students, I set a high goal for myself and volunteered to coordinate the new student orientation. This involved a formal program where I had to introduce the faculty and provide an overview of the school to entering students. The first year, I carefully scripted every word, practicing and timing the presentation almost to the second. Wearing a nice outfit, I confidently went to the front of the room. I looked at the audience, at my professors, at my fellow students, and froze. I looked down at my notes and read, never looking up. I was terrified, and the talk was a disaster.

So, what did I do? I kept practicing. I became the ALA student chapter president and led the meetings. I volunteered to be the library school representative for the university's graduate student association. I kept working at speaking and improved. The next year, I again volunteered to lead the new student orientation. I asked the dean for presentation tips, and he told me to start with a joke. This time, I didn't write everything down, although I did make an outline and practice. I began the presentation with a very silly joke (that hopefully no one remembers), and when everyone laughed, I immediately loosened up. It felt like the giant dividing line from before—between *me*, on the stage, and *them*, the audience—was gone. It felt like I was just having a conversation.

Viewing workshops as more like conversations than presentations is what has helped me most over the years. You can be personal; you can be yourself and be a lot more effective. I recently had a new trainer ask me for feedback. She said: "I know I have a really bouncy personality, should I try to tone it down?" I told her not to. I'd seen her train, and she was enthusiastic and fun. If she tried to tone it down, she would probably feel uncomfortable—and that would show.

I might be more personable in front of a classroom than I am on a regular basis. This is like going to a party where you don't know very many people. You may have to venture outside of your normal comfort zone in order to be truly "on" for the class, which does take a lot more energy than a normal conversation.

You can be yourself by incorporating stories and humor into your workshop. This sharing, though, should always relate to the topic. Don't just be a storyteller, but use your anecdotes to support the learning goals for the workshop. Anecdotes, analogies, stories, and examples can all help reinforce or clarify a point. You never have enough time in a workshop, so make every minute count toward helping the participants learn. For example, sharing personal experiences of how you have used the technology can help participants relate to the topic and understand how they can use it themselves. They will appreciate your keeping it real, and this can help you stay energized as well.

## Subject Knowledge

You don't have to have complete expertise; you don't have to have all the answers. You don't have to be an expert on blogs to teach an introductory class. You can always ask if others in the room know an answer if you don't. If none of you knows, offer to find the answer after class and follow up. You will, though, have to know something about a topic to teach about it. When creating any class, you have to do a little research, and you have to organize your knowledge in order to present it most effectively.

You can also partner with a subject matter expert (SME) to teach technology workshops. Technology trainer Brenda Hough organized a very successful one-hour workshop on "Investing on the Internet." Hough didn't know much about the topic, so she invited the president of a local investing club to present with her at the public library. The SME provided the investment expertise, and Hough taught the Internet skills. You could invite a healthcare professional to help teach a class about online medical resources, or have the historical society present a class on Internet genealogy.

Practice is important. Practice with a co-worker, your spouse, a friend, or at least in front of your mirror. This will help you with the timing of your delivery and in becoming more comfortable with your content.

## Empathy, Patience, and Flexibility

In *The Complete Computer Trainer,* Paul Clothier writes that: "[Computer training] is as much about empathy, patience, and respect as it is technical know-how."[1] When we were infants, we were constantly learning and trying new things. Some attempts succeeded; some failed. Infants fail all the time and don't mind. Adults, though, often have a fear of failure. This is one reason adults tend to have difficulty learning to use computers: They are scared they will do something wrong or that they will break the computer. Try to be as patient as possible, and just remember that this process may be intimidating. Try to be empathetic. Think back to the first time you drove a car, learned to swim, jumped from a plane, or mastered any other new and initially daunting skill. Let people explore and use the technology as much as possible during each workshop. When you let participants practice and make mistakes while you are there to help them, they are much more likely to actually use the technology when they leave. Be supportive and help them feel successful.

Flexibility is probably one of the best skills technology trainers can have. Gates Foundation trainers learned quickly that they could never have expectations about facilities, skill levels, or participant attitudes. You must "read" the participants and adjust the agenda if necessary; you won't always know their skill level in advance. Participants and their learning should always come first, not a preset list of contents.

To help you be more flexible, do your best to prepare for the unexpected. Think of questions or situations that might occur in your workshop, then brainstorm ideas on how you will deal with them. These, of course, include the training nightmares of a lost Internet connection, a broken projector, or even no electricity at all. When planning my wedding, I read a great tip: Just realize that *something* is going to go wrong, or at least not as you planned. If you go into a workshop thinking you can control every moment, you are sure to be not only disappointed but flustered. Some trainers give me a long list of "demands," which must be met in order for them to do their workshop. It is a great idea to ask for what you need, but always know that you can never completely count on all your requirements being met.

## Respect

I'll never forget one of my first experiences with another trainer on the job. She was a drill sergeant. She had an entire list of rules, and she enforced them. If two participants talked to each other, she would stop the class and go stand next to them until they stopped. The whole experience was intense and stressful. The next trainer I was teamed with, though, was the exact opposite. He sat down with the participants, made them comfortable, even joked with them throughout the training. He made sure they really understood and could demonstrate what they had learned about a topic before he moved on. In fact, they felt so comfortable that they even let him know when they needed a break because "their brains were full." He influenced their ability to learn by treating them with respect and as experienced adults with their own priorities.

Both mental and emotional factors build a great trainer. The first trainer didn't show much respect for the participants. Her first goal was to cover the material, but she didn't care about the people or about whether they really understood. Training should always be about people and their actual learning needs.

Demonstrate your respect by caring about the participants in your workshops—by caring about the quality of their time. Your audience should know up front that you are grateful for the time they are giving you, and you show that by being engaging, compelling, and interesting—or at least useful! You demonstrate it by assuming they are smart, by recognizing what they already bring to the discussion, and by neither insulting their intelligence nor ignoring their needs.

You should not only have respect for your participants, but you should encourage them to respect each other as well. In 1950, Knowles wrote in *Informal Adult Education* that training should help adults to "develop an attitude of acceptance, love, and respect toward others."[2] This does sound like something Miss America might be working on! But it really is true that a good workshop should include respectful discourse that distinguishes between people and ideas, and shows ways to challenge ideas without threatening people. This means that if someone is being rude to another participant, you will need to intervene. Addressing ground rules at the beginning of a workshop can be helpful in gaining collective buy-in.

Make sure your humor is respectful, both of the participants and of yourself. Don't overuse self-deprecating humor. I remember a trainer who would make jokes about how she was really overweight. Sure, the class laughed—but because they felt sorry for her and thought the least they could do was to laugh along with her. Jokes like this aren't good for your self-esteem, and people don't want to hear it. You can use jokes, but don't make them too personal. Laughing and acknowledging when you make a mistake or when you get an error message, though, can add a nice touch of humor. Be very careful about using a participant in a joke. You might be able to tease a little, but you never want to embarrass someone, no matter how confident they may appear.

Never put anyone in the spotlight who doesn't want to be there. I can think of nothing worse than picking a random participant to role-play in front of the room. This is terrifying for some people and uncomfortable for many others. Ask for volunteers, offer a reward (cheap prizes go far), but never, ever put someone up there who doesn't want to be! I've heard trainers say: "Well, they are adults, they can deal with it." Sure, they might be able to deal with it, but why make them? Terror does not inspire learning.

## Communication Skills

People are going to be listening to and watching you, so you need to be a good communicator. This means paying attention, not just to what you say, but to your body language, eye contact, voice quality, vocabulary, and listening skills. All of these aspects combine to convey your message.

One part of effective communication requires that you really listen to any questions from participants. After you answer, ask if your answer was helpful and if it covered everything they were asking.

Never interrupt someone asking a question, which sends the message that you don't *really* want participation. When I was a new technology trainer, I dreaded questions. A hand would go up, and I'd think: *Here comes an interruption; don't stop me now, I might lose my train of thought,* or *Oh, no, they're trying to stump me.* Now, I'm very grateful for participation, because I know that it is the best way for people to learn and share. You do have to be flexible, and you have to be very engaged, but questions can add excitement and interest to the workshop.

Read your audience and roll with the punches. I've seen many trainers who seem unaware of their participants and oblivious to what is going on. For example, a trainer once had her participants doing an exercise in small groups, and everyone was talking. She then told them to begin discussing the next topic. The two groups closest to her heard, but I could see that the other groups were involved in their own discussions and didn't hear her. She didn't check that each group understood. In this situation, it would have been better to go to each table individually or to make sure she had everyone's attention before giving new directions.

Of course, another part of communication skills involves the ability to adapt to different participants and how they communicate best. Some people are shy and will never ask a question in front of an entire room of people. You aren't going to get them over that fear in one workshop (or maybe even ever). Give them different ways they can communicate with you and with other participants. Before a break, you might ask if anyone has questions and be met with silence. Ten minutes into the break, you might find that four people have asked you a private question. That's OK; as a trainer, you don't really get a break! Break time is a great time for you to be available to the quieter participants, or even to deal with difficult participants, such as someone who is dominating the workshop with his or her own issues.

You can also encourage learners to answer your questions. When learners answer questions, it helps them process information. Putting answers into their own words helps reinforce their knowledge. Questioning techniques, especially critical thinking questions, are an easy way to help make your workshops more participatory. Ask learners to tell you what a next step would be, what the software could be used for, or about problems they've experienced before.

Use open-ended questions, those that require more than a yes or no answer. Don't just ask *Does everyone understand?* or *Are you ready for me to move on?* You'll probably just get mumbled responses. If they aren't ready to go on, or don't understand, they may be embarrassed to draw attention to themselves. Instead, ask, *What questions do you have on creating a blog?* or *What do you think you might use this tool for at home?* Then wait a full 10 seconds. This may seem like a long time, but participants need time to formulate their answers in their brains before they can speak.

Keep your communication style practical and easy-to-understand. Try not to assume previous knowledge or to use acronyms or unfamiliar vocabulary. This is helpful when marketing your workshops as well. Remember that not everyone will know what you mean when you use words like database, periodical, or library catalog, or will be unfamiliar with acronyms and brand names such as EBSCO, Medline, or OCLC.

Be explicit during guided instruction when directing attention to the screen or menu bars. Use directional language, such as stating that the *Start* button is in the lower left-hand corner. Older adults, especially, often look at the entire screen and prefer to examine everything on it first.

## Facilitation and Interaction

It is vital to develop good facilitation skills with both individuals and groups. Training is a partnership between the trainer and the participant, with learning as a shared goal. The first step in developing this skill is simple: Spend less time talking. Let participants do it for themselves. Again, be the "guide on the side, and not the sage on the stage." As General Ruben Cubero, U.S. Air Force Academy, puts it: "As you enter a classroom ask yourself this question: If there were no students in the room, could I do what I am planning to do? If your answer to the question is yes, don't do it" (serc.carleton.edu/sp/compadre/justintime/index.html).

When I first started learning and studying about how adults learn, I began incorporating group exercises into my workshops. This almost felt like I was cheating, like they were doing the work for me. It felt artificial. But I've learned that this is a balance. Let people share and explore, but don't make it seem contrived. Don't use a game just because it is fun or social; make sure it relates to the content. I once attended a workshop where there were so many silly games that I felt my time was being wasted. Try incorporating *one* game that reviews the material or reinforces the goals. Be careful about using an exercise just because you know it is time for one instead of to help the participants. You learn this as you go, and I still make mistakes. Sometimes, until you've tried an activity with a group, you can't really know how it will work out.

Don't make group work the only way you involve participants. I attended one workshop that incorporated too many group exercises, all of which involved group discussion. I ended up frustrated, tired of both my group and of making conversation. The trainer was very knowledgeable, and I really wanted him to share more of what he knew—but he didn't seem to contribute much to the workshop. Group work is not a good time for the trainer to take a break. This is the time for you to move from group to group, listen, address questions, and focus on individuals.

In the corporate world, trainers focus on performance-based training. This means that the outcome of their workshops will be a change in performance: a change in what someone can do, a change in their actions. This makes sense when you think about an employee doing mechanical work, but also when you think of someone using technology. For example, in a workshop on "Computer Troubleshooting," you wouldn't just teach participants about each part of the computer and what it does. They would also need to practice identifying symptoms, diagnosing common problems, and identifying causes. You would give them hands-on exercises and time to practice on their own.

Participants need to interact with the technology, with each other, and even with their own brains. Encourage independence. They need to practice and think things through themselves. Step-by-step instructions just won't stick in long-term memory. Giving participants time to do exercises on their own, or just time to explore, is another a way of learning. Also, try to give time for reflective thought so they can process information quietly.

## Planning Skills

Just like good librarians, good trainers are very organized. You need to plan two major components. First, you need to focus on the overall plan for technology training in your library to assess where training fits into your library services (covered in Chapter 7). Next, you need to plan and design your individual workshops (discussed in Chapter 8).

Technology training should build on the library's vision and strategic plan. It is important to determine training goals for the library that support the greater mission and that integrate technology training into existing library programs. Planning also involves determining target audiences, whose specific needs must be considered, and determining necessary resources, including space and technology.

Planning is imperative, whether training involves more formal classes or just one-on-one training in response to patron questions.

Many library trainers juggle their training responsibilities with other tasks such as reference work or technology support, so taking the time to plan may seem like a luxury. Don't, however, underestimate its importance.

## Delivery

A great way to improve your training is to tape or videotape your workshops. I know this might sound like a quick trip to hell, but in reality, it is extremely useful. I value Information Today, Inc.'s Computers in Libraries and Internet Librarian conferences, because they tape all the presenters. I've listened to two audiotapes of my presentations; I loved one, and one I really didn't. But by listening to both of them, I learned and improved. You can identify for yourself the areas in which you need improvement. I always find that, when I've thought my voice must be shaking, it really doesn't sound as bad as I thought! After all, we are usually our own worst critics.

When I helped coordinate train-the-trainer workshops for librarians, we videotaped trainers and let them watch their tapes independently. You can gain so much from watching a video of your training. One trainer came into class wearing a baseball cap. I thought about telling her she should take it off, but then decided that she would see it herself on the videotape. When she watched her tape, she realized that, when she sat behind the instructor computer station, the only thing visible to the class was the top three inches of her head—just her eyes and the baseball cap. It's not easy to make personal connections, let alone eye contact, that way. She will remember not to wear a cap in the future, though, since she saw the effects herself. This can be much more effective than if I had just told her how it looked.

Videotape can also help you to be aware of any unusual body language. Gestures and other visual elements can be distracting. I sometimes do a strange thing with my hand. I couldn't figure out why my wrist was always sore after workshops, until I saw myself in a video, turning and turning my hand in a circle. Even now, I sometimes catch myself doing this when I get really involved in a workshop, but I remember to check for it and try to stop.

You can also improve by studying how to use PowerPoint and other training tools effectively. A number of Web sites give tips, but much is logical if you think about each tool's purpose. For example, you don't want to include too much text on each PowerPoint slide—if you give your participants too much to read, they will have to stop listening to you to do so. By the same token, blinking text or a lot of moving images can be distracting. Think about what will help the participants learn. Flipcharts, for instance, are great for tracking ideas in a brainstorming session, but you should not get so involved with writing everything down that you miss what is being discussed or slow the pace of the workshop.

Chapter 8 goes into more detail about workshop design, but it all comes back to helping people learn. Keep your presentation logical and think about what participants would like to know when approaching the subject. I attended one workshop involving training on a statistical database where the trainer began by showing us how to build a report from scratch. It was difficult, and I can remember thinking, "but what would I use this report for?" I didn't know what I was working toward, so I wasn't really interested. If he had begun the workshop by showing us the end product, we would have understood the value of the reports before getting lost in the process.

Adults need to know what they are going to use the training for, what is in it for them. They need to know the context—how will they use this tool? Try to individualize their training experience as much as possible. You can do this by providing time for self-paced exercises, exploration time, or follow-up contact.

## Ten Tips to Quell the Qualms of Training

What about Glossophobia? No, this isn't a fear of shiny things or of lipgloss. Glossophobia (from the Greek *glosso,* meaning tongue) is a social phobia that includes the fear of speaking in public. It is said to be the single most common phobia, affecting as many as 75 percent of all people. Some studies show that people dread public speaking more than death! Most of us do have fears about speaking in public. Sure, you may hear that you should imagine the audience in their underwear, or that you can use that nervous energy for good, but it always helps me to think through concrete things that will help. These 10 tips will help quell the qualms of training:

1. Acknowledge that nervousness is normal.
2. Be aware of your breathing: Try not to breathe too quickly or too shallowly.
3. Remember that the participants want you to succeed.
4. Have a positive and confident outlook, even if you fake it at first!
5. Establish a warm-up routine/checklist. Get comfortable and familiar with the room, equipment, lights, etc.
6. Know as much as you can about your audience.
7. Practice and practice.
8. Focus on the people and your message, not your nerves.
9. Don't apologize or call attention to your nervousness.
10. Start with a relevant joke or story to make the content accessible.

Pay attention to comments on evaluation forms. When I was doing workshops in Seattle, I got so sick of seeing comments on the evaluation forms that I needed to speak louder. At first, I was in denial and blamed this on the noise of the computer lab, the whirring of the fans, the participants, the size of the room, or the acoustics. It was true that the background noise in the room was loud, and we installed sound panels eventually. But there were other trainers using that room, and their evaluations didn't ask them to speak up!

So, I set some improvement goals for myself and decided to see what could be done about my soft voice. I found a workshop series taught by a radio broadcaster on how to improve voice quality. I spent several weeks working with the instructor and learning how to project my voice and speak from my diaphragm. Now, talking loudly is easy for me, and I never get that comment on evaluation forms. You can improve, too. See Appendix C for a self-assessment checklist you can use to rate your training skills. Go to workshops yourself and learn from other trainers what to do and what not to do. Watch what works well and how they handle difficult participants or situations.

What exactly makes the difference between a good trainer and a great trainer? Some characteristics of good trainers include:

- Being flexible and adaptive to difficult situations

- Having excellent presentation and communication skills

- Designing and delivering training that addresses all learning styles (see Chapter 4)

- Knowing the content and keeping up-to-date on technology and training issues

- Being enthusiastic, engaging, and responsive to participants' ongoing needs

- Ensuring that learning occurs and effectively creating a learning community

- Modeling what is trained by example

Great trainers also incorporate extra preparation time, allow independent work, inspire others, and enable participants to succeed. This includes:

- Having backup plans in case of technology difficulties, and multiple independent exercise options

- Incorporating feedback, practicing new material, and customizing the workshop to each group

- Considering how to ensure that each participant's learning needs are met

- Updating and improving materials and subject matter based on participants' needs and technological changes

- Involving and inspiring participants and ensuring they can do it themselves

- Becoming experts and contributing to the library field by writing and training at conferences

- Ensuring participants can use the technology and following up after training

- Communicating in the style appropriate for the individual participant

- Ensuring participants are able to model their learning and showcase their work to others

Take the time to bring yourself from good to great!

## Endnotes

1. Paul Clothier, *The Complete Computer Trainer*, New York: McGraw-Hill, 1996: xvii.
2. Malcolm Shepherd Knowles, *Informal Adult Education: A Guide for Administrators, Leaders, and Teachers*, New York: Association Press, 1950: 9–10.

## Chapter 4

# Knowing Your Library Learners

*Tell me, I will forget. Show me, I may remember.*
*But involve me, and I will understand.*
                                        —Chinese Proverb

Learners vary in their interests, skill levels, ages, attitudes, motivation, and learning styles. When you know how different people learn best, you can plan and execute training most effectively.

What is the most important thing to know about how people learn? Diversity! This is what all the research really boils down to: Everyone learns differently. So, what can we as trainers do to help diverse individuals learn? We can involve the participants, and we can provide as much variety in the learning experience as possible. We can listen and support training participants, finding the ways to best respond to their needs. We can incorporate activities, discussions, exercises, and handouts that involve all types of learners.

## Learning Styles

Learning styles refer to the typical methods by which people take in and process information. Learning styles are the patterns of how you learn, solve problems, communicate, do your work, and interact with others. For example, when you give directions to someone, do you draw them a map or give them step-by-step instructions? When you meet people at a party, are you more likely to remember what they looked like or what you talked about? A number of things determine your learning style: past teachers and life experiences, how you were raised, hobbies, interests, and jobs. You may even prefer different learning styles depending on the topic.

We sometimes fall into the habit of training to our own learning style preferences. Adults, though, want trainers to teach to their own style. This helps them take in and process information more easily and to build on what they already know. Many of us have learned to learn from listening to lectures and reading, whether or not this truly fits our learning style. In a workshop, strive for a better balance so that all learning styles are addressed.

Try to find out as much as you can about the participants before the workshop. This isn't always possible, especially if you are just doing an hour-long public workshop, but the more information you have, the better. Some libraries even have participants fill out a brief survey when registering for a public workshop. When doing staff training, you probably have more access to this information. Here are some characteristics to try to identify:

- Demographics can be important, especially the age of the learners—adults, children, or teens.

- What are the existing skills of the participants?

- What are the participants' expectations regarding the training?

- Are the participants there by choice? How do they feel about attending (nervous, excited)?

- What are the other attributes of the learners? Are there particular strengths, limitations, or interests that may impact instruction?

- What are the learning-style preferences of the group? How will this impact the design/presentation of the material?

- What is the size of the group?

- Will this be a hands-on workshop? Will participants need to share computers?

- Do the participants have specific questions about the topic?

## Categories of Learning Styles

There are many different ways to categorize learning approaches. In fact, there are more than 50 different learning-style theories; there are also differences based on gender, generation, culture, and age. Educators, psychologists, and communication researchers all study learning styles. All agree that people take in the world differently, but they differ on how to categorize these differences. Since the majority of library technology workshops are designed for adult learners rather than for children, the following sections focus primarily on adults' learning styles.

### VAK Learning Style Preferences

Many common learning-style theories are based on sensory preferences, with broad categories that include Visual, Auditory, and Kinesthetic (VAK). Most interesting to realize here is that most people are kinesthetic or visual learners; very few are purely auditory. Yet, most college courses and many library workshops rely primarily on delivery by lecture, addressing only auditory learning styles. (Of course, most people do learn in several ways, but they tend to learn *best* through one or two predominant learning styles.)

How can you find out which type of learner you are and what kinds of learners you have in your workshop—especially if you don't know anything about them until they step in the door? Take note of your own preferences from the following descriptions and note also that they can give you clues that you can use during a workshop to figure out participants' learning styles:

- *Visual learners* – These learners gain knowledge best by seeing or reading what you're trying to teach. They need to see your body language and facial expressions to fully understand the content. They tend to prefer sitting at the front of the classroom to avoid visual obstructions. They may think in pictures and learn best from visual displays, such as flipcharts and demonstrations. They often prefer to take detailed notes to absorb the information and will appreciate handouts. They remember faces better than names.

- *Auditory learners* – These learners learn best through verbal lectures, discussions, talking things through, and listening to what others have to say. Auditory learners interpret the underlying meanings of speech through listening to tone of voice, pitch, speed, and other nuances. Written information may have little meaning. They can be easily distracted by outside noises or sounds. They may nod their head a lot when listening to a trainer. These learners often benefit from reading aloud. They remember names, but forget faces.

- *Kinesthetic learners* – These learners learn best through a hands-on approach, actively exploring the physical world around them. They often ignore instruction manuals, instead jumping right in and trying things out on their own. They may find it hard to sit still for long periods, and may become distracted and have a hard time concentrating on a lecture. They enjoy activities, group work, and self-paced exercises. They may doodle or appreciate having toys to manipulate while in a workshop. They may gesture a lot when talking. They have a difficult time remembering faces and names, but can often remember entire conversations.

These wide varieties in learning styles require you to present material using several different methods. For example, if you want students to learn how to create a resume in Microsoft Word, start by showing a completed example. Then, explain the process, let them write down the basics they want to include, brainstorm together what kind of information usually appears on a resume, give them some written directions, and then let them work on their own computers. Throughout, use questioning techniques to get them communicating and talking.

## Knowles and Adult Learners

Malcolm Knowles, who has been called the father of adult education, articulated the principles of adult learning after working with adults and observing the ways in which they learned best. He used the term "andragogy" to describe the distinctive ways in which adults learn. "Andragogy" and "pedagogy" refer to the study of teaching, "*andra*" meaning "man, adult" and "*peda*" meaning "child."

Adults really do learn differently than children—they aren't just big kids (though sometimes you might think otherwise!). Adults learn best:

- When they can be self-directed and have a say in what they will learn
- When they can relate and build on their own experiences
- When they have a need to learn and are motivated
- When they know why something is important to learn, why it is relevant
- When they can apply new knowledge and skills immediately

Each adult is different. Each has different needs, and these needs are constantly changing. Adults have a need for economic, social, and psychological security. They have a need for recognition, for affection, for acceptance. They need to feel useful and appreciated.

What can you do as a trainer to support adult learners?

- Break up content into "bite-size chunks," which people are able to understand easily

- Try to find out and alleviate any concerns they have regarding the workshop

- Let them know at the beginning of the workshop that you will incorporate their experience and that you want to meet their needs

- Show the whole picture/end product, followed by the details, and then give a refresher with the overall picture

- Show the relevance of the subject matter, demonstrate how they will actually use it

- Explain *why* activities are used and their relevance to the overall course or training session

- Provide plenty of hands-on experience, with opportunities for success and praise

- Incorporate small-group work, since participants will be more likely to converse and ask each other for assistance rather than ask the trainer in front of the group

- Give them some choices by providing options and flexibility in their self-directed activities

- Create a climate of exploration and encourage them to have a go at it themselves

- Keep the learning objectives in perspective to the amount of time for the workshop; don't try to cover more material than they can actually learn

- Make certain participants are equipped with enough knowledge and skill to complete any task, rather than setting them up for failure

- Bend the rules, if necessary and appropriate; try new things and adjust to the participants' needs

### Kolb and Experiential Learning

David Kolb, a leading researcher in learning strategies and learning processes, has focused his work on experiential learning. This learner-centered approach starts with the premise that people learn best from experience ("learning by doing"). Kolb theorized that people have different preferences for learning styles in the same way that they have different preferences when it comes to their chosen occupations. He noticed that, during a given training experience, some participants preferred certain activities, finding them very useful, while other people disliked these same activities and were dissatisfied.

Kolb created a cycle to represent the learning process. The four parts of the learning cycle are:

- Concrete experience (following exercises, observations, step-by-step directions)

- Reflective observation (journaling, brainstorming, studying)

- Abstract conceptualization (lecturing, writing, using analogies, thinking)

- Active experimentation (simulations, case studies, planning, testing)

The learning cycle doesn't follow an exact order. Rather, workshops should be designed to include the learning cycle of experiencing, reflecting, thinking, and acting so that every type of learner has a way to connect with the material. You can combine the parts of the cycle throughout a workshop.

Kolb's four learning styles each combine two parts of the learning cycle. Again, what you really want to do is design so that there is some way for those with every learning style to engage with the topic. Kolb's four learning styles are:

- Diverging: combines preferences for *experiencing* and *reflecting*

- Assimilating: combines preferences for *reflecting* and *thinking*

- Converging: combines preferences for *thinking* and *doing*

- Accommodating: combines preferences for *doing* and *experiencing*

Experiential learning recognizes that people learn best from their own experiences and their own interpretations. What people do is more important than what they know. A learning experience can increase people's learning and retention of new knowledge and skills. The learning process should be enjoyable, motivating, and rewarding. Everyone's ideas and choices should be respected, and opportunities should be provided for people to take on challenges in an atmosphere of support. Provide time for reflection and the realization that an attempt at something new or different is more significant than the immediate result.

### Felder and Soloman's Learning-Style Model

Two professors at North Carolina State University, Richard Felder and Barbara Soloman, formulated a learning strategy that involves four dimensions: sensing/intuitive, visual/verbal, active/reflective, and sequential/global. The differences in these styles include:

- *Sensing learners* are concrete, practical, and oriented toward facts and procedures. *Intuitive learners* are conceptual, innovative, and oriented toward theories and meanings.

- *Visual learners* prefer visual representations of presented material—pictures, diagrams, flow charts, etc. *Verbal learners* prefer written and spoken explanations.

- *Active learners* learn by trying things out and prefer to work with others. *Reflective learners* learn by thinking things through and prefer to work alone.

- *Sequential learners* are linear and orderly; they usually learn in small incremental steps. *Global learners* are holistic, systems thinkers; they tend to learn in large leaps.

The free *Index of Learning Styles* (www.ncsu.edu/felder-public/ILSpage.html; click on "ILS Questionnaire") is an online assessment that you can use to determine your learning styles according to this model. (Some questions do deal more with typical student work, such as test taking or learning in a classroom.)

### Myers-Briggs Type Inventory

The Myers-Briggs Type Inventory (MBTI) is a popular instrument based on the theories of Carl Jung. It measures four preferences (introvert/extrovert, intuitive/sensing, thinking/feeling, and judging/perceiving) and equates 16 personality types. These preferences identify how you prefer to process and organize information, direct your energy, make decisions, and manage your life. There are many sources for studying more about this tool, and the Myers & Briggs Foundation (www.myersbriggs.org) can provide you with resources on assessments.

### McCarthy's 4Mat System

Bernice McCarthy described four types of learners: innovative, analytic, common sense, and dynamic. She proposed the 4Mat

System, which is described as a spiral process of learning. To use this process, you would begin a workshop with a right brain, structured activity designed for motivational arousal. This would be a sensing/feeling activity that would appeal to innovative learners. The next component would be an intellectual activity, geared toward analytic learners. Participants would then practice working on a hands-on activity, personalized to the individual if possible. Finally, participants would be given activities that would apply to real-world situations.

*Innovative learners:*
- look for personal meaning while learning
- draw on their values while learning, like to share opinions and beliefs
- enjoy social interaction, like group activities

*Analytic learners:*
- want to develop intellectually while learning
- prefer facts
- are patient and reflective
- want to know "important things" and to add to the world's knowledge

*Common sense learners:*
- want to find solutions and like problem-solving activities
- value things if they are useful
- are kinesthetic
- are practical and straightforward
- want to make things happen

*Dynamic learners:*
- look for hidden possibilities

- judge things by gut reactions and feelings

- synthesize information from different sources

- are enthusiastic and adventurous, prefer challenging activities

## How to Address Learning Preferences in Training

By now, it should be clear that workshop participants will have different ways of learning best. So, what can you do as a trainer to bridge these differences? Although there are many learning-style models to choose from, simply take away one important message: Adults learn in different ways. This may be in 1) the type of information they learn best—analytical, conceptual, or artistic; 2) the way they learn best—seeing, hearing, or doing; or 3) the preferred learning strategy—learning by intuition, perception, thinking, doing.

Learn to expect this. Know that your participants will process information differently and try to plan for the different styles. Try to find out as much as you can about the participants; look for ways to link the content to their interests, their backgrounds, and the ways in which they will be using the knowledge. Your efforts will help them remember.

Adult learners bring their own skills, interests, and experiences to the workshop. These experiences can influence how learners perceive training—and can lead to apprehension, misconceptions, biases, and defensiveness. Even their lack of knowledge on a subject may cause vulnerabilities. But, they all have a desire to learn. Adult learners are motivated, and they have an objective in mind—or they wouldn't have come to your workshop. Find out what their objectives are. Workshops are often designed based on what the trainer or a committee thinks people should know, rather than what they really want or need to learn.

Be creative. Use PowerPoint presentations, flipcharts, white-boards, objects (props, electronic devices, etc.), handouts, exercises, decorations, videos, role-playing, demonstrations, and discussions. Spend more time facilitating exercises than lecturing, and be sure to plan enough time for application and practice. Learners have to be able to "do it" for themselves. Allow time for them to practice using a given tool, in their own context. For example, in my class on Emerging Technologies, I give attendees time to explore a few online social networking tools of their choice in depth. If they practice making a blog, they will understand it more thoroughly than if they just watch you do it. (If they are more advanced, they can create a wiki!)

## Generational Differences

It isn't surprising to find three or four generations in one technology workshop. Generational differences will affect how participants learn and also how they interact with you and each other. A 2000 human resources article, "Solutions for Training Today's Age Diverse Workforce," brought up a few good points. First, Generation Xers (my generation, born between 1965 and 1977), have not only the ability to "focus on several things at once," but also the ability to "selectively eliminate what they don't need from what they truly need."[1] I suppose this is why work/life balance is such a popular goal and perhaps why I hear fewer complaints about the difficulty keeping up with new technologies from those in Generations X and Y.

But, what does this mean for training? Generational differences just mean that we need to include the same variety and opportunities for independence into our workshops that we do to meet the needs of different learning styles. It is true that Baby Boomers might seem to pay better attention to me in a workshop. It may be, though, that they are just being polite and appearing to pay attention, while all the while writing to-do lists in the margin of their worksheets instead of overtly checking their e-mails as a 20-something might. Think about what each age group would be interested in. Twenty-year-olds might be interested in learning social skills, then job related or family skills, while Boomers might be interested in community affairs and preparing for purposeful retirement.

Children learn differently because they have not yet had many experiences, so they do not need to relate what they are learning to existing knowledge. Children learn more through trial and error, and are less afraid to keep trying and testing. They are also more satisfied when a trainer tells them they will use the information in the future; they do not need the proof that adults need. Children often follow directions better, need repetitive instruction, and may be influenced by peer pressure. However, they do resemble adults who learn best through hands-on work, with free time to explore and practice time in a safe, supportive learning environment.

## The Memory Dilemma

When we receive information, it first passes quickly through our perception filters. We determine whether this is something of which we need to be aware. Information then moves into short-term memory, where it is considered, and either discarded or passed to our long-term memory. Our short-term memory is sort of a buffer zone in which small chunks of information are temporarily held. The challenge for trainers is to get information into participants' long-term memory, so that learners can build the necessary neural networks to ensure information can be retrieved later.

Studies show that 70 percent of the information presented within the first 10 minutes of a lecture is retained; however, this quickly drops to 20 percent for the remainder of the presentation.

Learners become disengaged, and the information then is, for the most part, lost. Considering this, we should spend more time planning *how* information is delivered (so that we can keep learners engaged and learning), rather than just planning what we will say.

Consider the typical PowerPoint presentation with lecture: many slides, crammed with many bullet points, and a talking head. We've all experienced such workshops, in which the objective seems to be to get through all of the speaker's information within the allotted time. There is no participant engagement.

If the objective is learning, rather than lecturing, workshops need to be less concerned with content and more concerned with learners' ability to retain what is presented. This is not to say that content is unimportant—the challenge, however, is to deliver content in such a way that it can be absorbed. Engagement requires strategies that promote processing rather than memorizing information so that participants retain knowledge and deeper conceptual insights. Think about the average retention percentages for various instructional methods:

- Lecture = 5 percent
- Reading = 10 percent
- Audiovisual = 20 percent
- Demonstration = 30 percent
- Discussion group = 50 percent
- Practice by doing = 75 percent
- Teach others/immediate use of learning = 90 percent

We really do learn and retain best when we are able to have an experience and not just read or sit through a lecture. People create meaning through interactions with each other and by actually practicing and doing something themselves. Learning that is

processed in participants' brains when they do an activity themselves will help them make that transfer from short-term to long-
term memory.

## Endnotes

1.  Bruce Tulgan, "Solutions for Training Today's Age Diverse Workforce,"
    *HRfocus*, January 2000: 6.

Chapter 5

# Learning Interactively

*Learning is not a spectator sport.*
                                        —Donald Blocher

During any workshop, it is very important to use hands-on activities to ensure that learning not only happens, but is retained. The best way to learn is by doing. Participants who are able to demonstrate what they've learned, in their own words or by doing it themselves, are much more likely to retain their new knowledge in long-term memory. In *The Ten-Minute Trainer*, Bowman writes: "According to educational research, most learners only remember about 10 percent of what they read. If they interact with the written information in some way, the probability increases that learners will remember more."[1]

While working for the Bill & Melinda Gates Foundation, I met one librarian who originally worked in reference—but because she knew a lot about computers, her library director decided she should become a technology trainer (imagine that!). At first, she was really upset with the prospect of having to train. She had gone to school to learn how to do research, to be a librarian. She knew she was good at that, but didn't know anything about training. Her husband was actually a high school teacher who had been educated on teaching methods; in contrast, she felt very much unprepared for assuming such a new responsibility.

At first, she basically felt that her job was to entertain a room full of strangers for an hour. But then she found out about interactive training. This changed how she felt about training because it shifted the responsibility for learning to the students. People learn better when actively involved; your participants will retain the information they learn and will be more interested in your workshops.

## Using Activities

Whether it is called active learning, accelerated learning, interactive learning, self-directed learning, or engaged learning, the basic principles and techniques remain constant. While there are some differences between the methods, the underlying techniques are united in the practice of promoting learning new ideas, skills, and attitudes through doing, performing, or taking an action. The process combines adult learning theory and whole brain learning theory to achieve a faster learning rate. It involves the use of techniques such as group discussion, learning games, simulations, reflection, and role-playing.

Active learning refers to anything in a class that engages students with the material being presented. Participants might be called on to work individually or in small groups for brief periods of time to answer questions, start problem solutions, fill in steps in a problem solution or derivation, brainstorm lists, troubleshoot processes, or think of questions about the material just lectured on. At the end of the allotted period, the trainer calls on several individuals or teams for their responses, collects more responses from volunteers, then moves on when the correct answer has been obtained—and it seems clear that students understand it.

Interactive learning describes a method of acquiring information through hands-on, interactive means. The opposite of interactive learning is passive learning, which involves merely observing a learning process or just listening to information. Interactive learning is commonly employed in schools today and often involves the use of computers and other tangible equipment.

Activity refocuses participants who have drifted off into mental breaks and energizes the entire class. Encouraging independence empowers participants. They are able to make their mistakes while the trainer is still present to provide assistance, instead of when the training is over. This can be one of the most difficult things for a new library trainer to understand, but can completely change how they train, increasing the odds of success for the trainer and the participants.

Although mistakes are an important part of learning, no one really wants to fail. Make sure you build in opportunities for success, which allow participants to develop their skills. Success helps promote initiative, a sense of achievement, and confidence. In *The Ten-Minute Trainer*, Bowman says that activities RAP up the learning, giving participants an opportunity to **R**einforce, **A**pply, and **P**ractice what has been learned.[2]

A self-directed learner has responsibility for what he or she learns. The trainer is not a presenter, but a facilitator who involves the learner in locating the resources necessary for learning. The point isn't to offer entertainment, but to present library resources in an accessible, appealing, and understandable format.

In Mel Silberman's *Training the Active Training Way*, each chapter conveys a strategy for active learning.[3] These eight strategies are:

1. Engage Your Participants from the Start

2. Be a Brain-Friendly Presenter

3. Encourage Lively and Focused Discussion

4. Urge Participants to Ask Questions

5. Let Participants Learn from Each Other

6. Enhance Learning by Experience and Doing

7. Blend in Technology Wisely

8. Make the End Unforgettable

## Icebreakers

To break the ice, or not to break the ice … There is some controversy about the use of icebreakers in the training world. Some experts can't imagine not using them, while others view them as just fluff. I'm right in the middle of the road on that debate. Some icebreakers are silly and last too long, but I do think that there is merit in giving participants an opportunity to focus on the topic and have their first interaction with the group. This is also a great time to find out why they are there and what it is they want to learn, helping you to match the workshop to their needs.

Icebreaker purposes include:

- Allows participants to move and interact with different people
- Alleviates tension
- Creates group bonding—everyone is in the same situation
- Lets everyone get to speak for the first time
- Sets a tone of engagement
- Uses creative thinking
- Provides an introduction to the topic

An icebreaker is usually a fun and fast activity at the beginning of a training session that helps people relax, get to know each other, and become introduced to the training material. You can use polling or voting, pairs or small groups, or play a game. By using an icebreaker, you begin to create the interactive community that sustains active learning.

## Examples of Learning Interactivities

Use activities to find out the needs, expectations, and concerns of the participants so that you can gear instruction appropriately.

You can help them learn through doing and also check that learning is occurring throughout the workshop. There are a variety of ways to structure discussion and to obtain responses from participants during a session. You can obtain answers through open discussion, a go-around, response cards, polling, and games. Some methods are especially suitable when time is limited or participation needs to be coaxed. You might also consider combining a few activities.

Provide very clear instructions, and try to present details in multiple formats. For example, give instructions on a handout, on a PowerPoint slide, on a flipchart, *and* verbally. Don't keep talking when people are working; talking over group work will go unheard. Here are a few inventive activity ideas:

- *Pair Share or Learning Partners* – This activity involves participants sharing information with a partner. They can brainstorm answers on a question about the topic, share the most important thing they learned with each other, practice a skill, test each other, show each other what they have created (a blog, a PowerPoint show, a resume), or tell each other how they are going to apply what they learned.

- *Action Plans* – Participants make an action plan for themselves on what steps they will take to use the information learned in the workshop. These action plans can be kept to themselves; they can just write down two or three ways they will use the information they've learned. Or they can share these plans with another participant or a small group.

- *Question Sharing* – Sometimes participants are reluctant to ask questions in front of the entire group. You can use a number of exercises to make it easier and less intimidating for them to find out answers. This could be as simple as having them write down two questions on an index card and pass the cards to the front. Then, you could pick some to share with the group, or you could form small groups and give each group a set of questions to answer together. Alternatively, you could collect the questions and answers at the end of class and e-mail the entire set to the participants.

- *Snowball Fight* – Participants write down a question about the material (or, alternatively, a statement about what they've learned) and then crumple the paper into a ball. The trainer gives a signal and they stand and throw their "snowballs." All snowballs should be kept in movement for a few minutes. When one falls, participants pick it up and throw it again. Stop the action and ask everyone to pick up a "snowball." Give the participants three minutes to read the question and find the answer using any-one or anything in the room as a resource. Then, have participants read the question and answer aloud or share with a small group. I used this during a conference presentation at the Hawaii Library Association, so we actually had a snowball fight in Hawaii!

- *Musical Questions* – Give each participant an index card and ask them to write down a question related to the workshop topic. While sitting in chairs or standing in a large circle, play music, asking them to keep passing their question cards to the right until the music stops. When the music stops, give them three to five minutes to research the answer to the question they are holding, using any person or resource available. Then debrief by having each participant read their question and answer. If you have a large group, you can just ask for a few volunteers to read aloud.

- *Scavenger Hunt* – This one is from Max Anderson, Educational Services Librarian, SOLINET, Atlanta (GA): "I teach classes about searching (whether it be OCLC, or even Web searching). At the beginning of these classes, the students are given a quick set of items to search for without any real knowledge of how to do the searches, and they are timed. Then, at the end of the class, the students do the same timed exercise. Based on the difference in how long it took them at the beginning vs. the end of class, they get a rudimentary idea of how their efficiency improved based on what they learned. This idea is also used in promotion of classes (e.g., 'students who took this class were an average of 40 percent more efficient at searching in OCLC than before they took the class')."

- *Pop-Ups* – In *The Ten-Minute Trainer*, Bowman gives many examples of interactivities, including "Pop-Ups."[4] Tell participants that a Pop-Up is when participants pop out of their chairs and state what they plan to do with what they learned. You could specify, for example, that in order to get three (or five) extra lunchtime minutes, 15 Pop-Ups are needed from the group in 60 seconds. This would be a great review, especially in the afternoon when energy is low—and it could be used to add minutes to an afternoon break.

- *Top 10 Lists* – I always love making top 10 lists. There are a number of ways to use these lists, such as 10 important things to remember or 10 ways to use the software. You could have participants form a group and list the items to be included in a top 10 on a flipchart. Then, have them "vote" on their favorites during a break by placing colored stickers or dots next to their personal preferences. Or have them work on their own to read a list of bulleted items you have created and mark the three they find most useful. This will ensure they read the list and process the information for themselves.

- *Postcard Partners* – Bowman describes this icebreaker in *The Ten-Minute Trainer*.[5] Buy various postcards and write a question or issue related to the workshop topic on the back. Cut each postcard in thirds, trying to make each set unique, and mix up the pieces. As participants come in the room, they each choose a postcard piece. When everyone has arrived, have participants find their partners by comparing postcard pieces until they find a match. Give them a few minutes to discuss the question or statement from their recreated postcard and introduce themselves. If you have time, you can have the participants report to the entire group and include the reasons they are interested in the workshop topic. You could also do this as a review activity, with participants creating their own postcards.

- *Postcard Follow-up* – Using postcards or notes, have participants write a note to themselves with things they want to remember or do regarding the topic. Then, mail the postcards to them a few weeks later as a follow-up activity.

- *Chocolate Hugs and Kisses* – Give a Hershey's Kiss to a learner who asks a question or makes a good point. Give a Hershey's Hug to someone who is having trouble with an exercise, gets discouraged, or crashes the computer.

- *Help!* – Some participants find it difficult to ask for help when doing self-directed exercises. Also, sometimes it is hard for a trainer to keep track of who needs assistance if several participants get stuck while working on their own. There are a few ways to make this easier. One is to decorate plastic cups (this could be as simple as writing "HELP" with a marker) and place one next to each computer. When participants have a question or get stuck during an exercise, they place their cup on top of the computer. This lets the trainer know they need assistance while avoiding participant embarrassment. A variation on this is to make a paper mailbox flag and tape it to the side of the computer screen. When people need help, they raise the flag.

- *Quick Guides* – Divide participants into teams to produce a one-page quick tip sheet related to the class. Let them use the computer or just use paper and colored pens.

- *Team Quizzes* – Divide the class into teams. Each team is responsible for creating a quiz related to the workshop. Once the quiz is completed, have the teams switch quizzes and give them 10 minutes to answer the questions. The team that finishes first wins. This serves as a great review exercise.

- *Grab that Spoon!* – Bowman describes the following game in *The Ten-Minute Trainer*.[6] Each participant writes a review question and answer related to the workshop topic on an index card. They are to write a point value (from one to 10) for the question, with one being an easy question and 10 being a very tough question. Then, form groups of four to five people and place a plastic spoon, toy, or computer mouse in the middle of the table. One person in the group reads his question to the group, and the member who grabs the toy first tries to answer the question. If they are correct, they get the point value on the card. If incorrect, they lose that amount of points or stay at zero points. The reader may not answer his own question. At the end of five minutes, the person with the most points wins. You can award small prizes for winners and consolation prizes for losers or just have the winners individually announced and applauded.

- *Polling* – This is really fun during online training and can be used in person as well. Verbally poll participants by a raise of hand or answer cards, or hand out a short survey at the workshop. Use polling to quickly assess participants' skills or interests. You can also start a discussion with a poll. For example, follow up on *Raise your hand if you have used Excel before* by asking those with their hands up how they have used the program. If you use a written survey, try to give the results as quickly as possible.

- *Simile Creation* – Metaphors and similes are often used in technology training to relate technology to objects or events with which participants are more familiar. Examples include comparing the feeling of using a computer for the first time to the experience of driving a car for the first time; or, similarly, not having to know how a computer works to use it, just like you might not know how a car works, but can still drive. Have the participants come up with a metaphor to describe some concept of the workshop topic or technology. This can be more imaginative if you assign them an unrelated object, such as "____ is like an eraser because …"; or "____ is like traveling because …"; or "____ is like a broom because …" An example answer would be: "Searching on the Internet is like traveling because you explore, find new things every day, and sometimes get lost."

- *World Café* – This interactive group activity is great for creating conversation on an important issue, centered on a single discussion question. All instructions are included in Café to Go, a free six-page guide available online (theworldcafe.com/twcrg.html). Some libraries have used this exercise as an entire program to host community conversations or to generate staff dialogue.

- *Quotations* – Create a simple PowerPoint presentation with quotations or cartoons related to your training. Ask each person to pick a favorite and tell another participant or the group why it is their favorite.

- *2 Truths and a Lie* – Max Anderson, Educational Services Librarian, SOLINET, Atlanta (GA), uses a variation on this exercise, which can also be used as a small group activity. "Each participant has to stand up and say three things about themselves. One of the things is a lie. The other participants are given the opportunity to vote on what they think is the lie. It is usually a lot of fun and breaks any initial tension they feel."

- *I feel like …* – Have each participant tell the class (or their table or neighbor) what animal or object they currently feel like and why. You can create a list to give them ideas, if necessary. For example, they may feel like popcorn because they are bursting with energy; or they may feel like a Popsicle because the room is too cold; or they may feel like a dinosaur because they are behind on emerging technologies.

- *Pre-assessment E-mail* – Have participants e-mail you before the workshop with five things they want to get out of the training, questions they have, and/or skills they wish to learn. This will let you know their expectations before the workshop begins.

- *Bingo!* – Create a Bingo card with squares in a grid. In each square, include a question, technology term, or personal fact. Participants have others in the room sign a square if they can answer the question or meet the criterion. Some examples include: Find someone who has the same birthday month as you do; has the same type of pet; has an MP3 player; knows one way to limit an Internet search; knows one Web site to search for book recommendations; has a blog; likes coffee.

- *Pictionary* – Write terms related to the training topic on index cards. Divide the participants into several groups. One person selects a card, and, without speaking, draws the term while the other team members guess the term. The first team to finish all terms wins.

- *Jeopardy* – Based on the popular television game show, this is one of my favorite review activities. Choose several categories related to your technology topic, such as Definitions, Acronyms, PowerPoint Tips, Internet Tools, and Potpourri. Create questions and answers that correspond to these categories (or have participants create these and submit them to you). Depending on the length of time you want to give for this activity, you may have about three categories with five questions under each category. Participants form teams. The answers are given, and participants must provide the accompanying question. More points are awarded for more difficult questions. This learning game usually creates a lot of excitement and fun competition. I use PowerPoint to display the categories, point values, answers, and questions. You could also display the game using cards, flipcharts, or even a whiteboard.

## Designing Activities

Because people forget most of what they hear, trainers must help facilitate learning experiences by using activities in workshops. You can't learn for participants; they have to experience learning themselves. A hands-on computer class will always be more effective than a lecture or demonstration.

When you choose types of activities, consider what knowledge and skills you want the participants to have at the end of the workshop. Do not just keep participants busy, but make sure activities promote deeper learning. The fundamental idea underlying engagement theory is that participants must be meaningfully engaged in learning activities through interaction with others and worthwhile tasks. All activities should involve active cognitive processes such as creating, problem solving, reasoning, decision making, and evaluation. Active training cannot occur without the involvement of participants.

As Roy Tennant writes in *Library Journal:* "Learn all the time without even thinking about it. We are born to learn, but somewhere along the way many of us pick up the idea that we must be taught in order to learn. We think that if someone doesn't stand up in front of us and talk to us with either a chalkboard or PowerPoint slides, we cannot learn. We must regain our sense of wonder and our desire to learn."[7] With the use of interactive learning techniques, you can help your participants remember the joy of exploring, discovering, and just being excited about learning.

Two expert trainers interviewed for this book provide wise advice:

*Michael Stephens, Instructor, Graduate School of Library & Information Science at Dominican University, River Forest (IL)* – "Librarians need to let go of the culture of perfect (those that still hold on to it) and look at what the gamers have learned: Try, try again and learn from it … Hand in hand with experience, comes PLAY. Let's make this stuff fun. Try Second Life for the experience and to FLY! It's just plain fun. Ponder how you'll play this coming year. Will it be your library's Learning 2.0 program? Will it be shooting some fun pics for the library Flickr account? Is it building and participating in a virtual community that lives on your library server, devoted to a love of reading, film group or knitting? Whatever it is—HAVE FUN."

*Mary Bucher Ross, training consultant, Seattle (WA)* – "I use many questioning techniques to involve learners. My favorite is to ask a closed question, followed by an open question. Here's how it works: I ask, 'How many of you have used Librarian's Internet Index as the starting point for a search?' Then I wait for hands to be raised and address the next question to someone who has raised his/her hand. 'Paul, when do you find LII to be an effective starting point?' By using the closed question first, I know who is paying attention and who has experience to contribute. Then, I can draw out someone who may have been more reluctant to volunteer this experience."

## Endnotes

1. Sharon L. Bowman, *The Ten-Minute Trainer: 150 Ways to Teach It Quick and Make It Stick!* San Francisco, CA: Pfeiffer, 2005: 59.
2. Bowman, 62.
3. Melvin L. Silberman, *Training the Active Training Way,* San Francisco, CA: Pfeiffer, 2006.
4. Bowman, 84.
5. Bowman, 102–104.
6. Bowman, 152.
7. Roy Tennant, "Strategies for Keeping Current," , Sept. 15, 2003: 28.

## Chapter 6

# Creating and Maintaining Interest

*Education's purpose is to replace an empty mind
with an open one.*

—Malcolm S. Forbes

Training strategies often overlook the role of motivation and the importance of maintaining interest, but these can be two of the most critical elements for success. Learning and retention cannot happen if you lose the participants' attention. Trainers need to make their workshops interesting, without making them purely entertaining.

## Motivation

For a while now, I've been fascinated by books about marketing, but wasn't sure exactly why. I knew I had an interest in marketing library services and in ways to sell libraries to funders for grants and other monetary support, and I did enjoy inventive marketing techniques—but then it finally hit me. Both training and marketing have to do with motivation and creating a change in a person. Marketing may motivate a consumer to believe in and buy a product, where training is about motivating a learner to believe in and buy-in to knowledge. You have to attract them to your training and keep them interested. They must be satisfied with the product (what they learn) well enough to go home and actually use it.

As expert trainer Mary Bucher Ross wrote in the survey for this book, "I think that a trainer must provide WIIFM and YCDI for the learners—that's, 'What's in it for me' and 'You can do it.' We have to help learners realize how these new skills are useful and relevant for their needs and that they will be successful in their learning."

Everyone is motivated by personal desires, interests, and goals. But what, specifically, motivates people to learn? A mandate from their boss? Personal learning goals? A feeling of satisfaction in knowing something new that will help you do a job better and more efficiently? Motivation is having the desire and willingness to do something. Motivation is mostly internal, based on what is important to the individual. A motivated person can be reaching for a long-term goal, such as becoming a professional writer, or a more short-term goal, such as learning how to create a blog.

There are two kinds of motivation:

- *Intrinsic motivation* occurs when people are internally motivated to do something because it brings them pleasure, they view it as important, or they consider what they are learning as morally significant. This would include an internal desire to learn, such as in lifelong learners, and also feelings of obligation, needs for satisfaction or accomplishment, or even interest related to hobbies.

- *Extrinsic motivation* occurs when a person is compelled to do something or act a certain way because of external factors, such as money, good grades, a promotion, praise, incentives, or rewards.

Internal motivation is usually stronger than external. For example, studies show that people value job satisfaction over high salaries and promotions. (Certainly, the library field seems to demonstrate this theory.)

The following sections examine a few theories of motivation. The first, Maslow's theory, is a theory of human innate needs, while the second, McClelland's theory of learned needs, focuses on those needs acquired through experiences. Lastly, we will explore the ARCS Motivation Model to pull these theories together for training purposes.

### Maslow's Theory of Human Needs

Abraham Maslow's humanistic hierarchy of human needs theory, published in 1943, is one of the most widely discussed theories of motivation. His hiearchy was based originally on five needs. These needs, listed from basic (lowest) to most complex (highest), are: 1) physiological, 2) safety, 3) social, 4) esteem, and 5) self-actualization (see Figure 6.1).

All of the first four levels Maslow named are deficit needs. In other words, they cease to be motivating when fulfilled. For example, if you are thirsty, you are motivated to find something to drink;

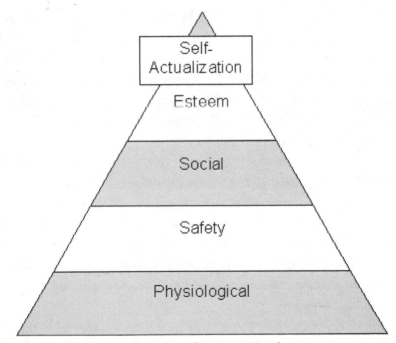

Figure 6.1　Maslow's Hierarchy of Human Needs

if you aren't thirsty, you don't feel any thirst motivation. According to Maslow, an individual is ready to act upon the growth needs if and only if the deficiency needs are met. His theory includes the following conclusions:

- Human beings have wants and desires that influence their behavior. Only unsatisfied needs influence behavior; satisfied needs do not.

- Since there are many needs, they are arranged in order of importance, from the basic to the complex.

- A person can only advance to the next level of needs after the lower level need is at least minimally satisfied.

- The higher up the hierarchy a person is, the more individuality, humanity, and psychological health they will demonstrate.

Maslow's initial conceptualization included only one growth need: self-actualization. Self-actualized people are characterized by: 1) being problem-focused, 2) incorporating an ongoing freshness of appreciation of life, 3) showing a concern about personal growth, and 4) having the ability to have peak experiences. There is some debate as to the validity of the hierachy of the needs, and Maslow later added the cognitive desires (to know, to understand, and to explore); the aesthetic needs (for beauty, art, and order); and transcendence (helping others to achieve their potential).

Maslow's basic position is that, as one becomes more self-actualized and transcendent, one becomes more wise (develops wisdom) and automatically knows what to do in a wide variety of situations. Self-actualization deals with personal growth and fulfillment, making the most of your abilities and striving for personal improvement.

Here, the important thing to remember as a trainer is that if people are focused on fulfilling their basic needs, they cannot concentrate on higher level aspirations such as learning and knowledge building. Make certain you do everything you can to address the deficit needs. Table 6.1 shows a few examples of what you can provide to help participants focus on their higher level needs.

Table 6.1  Participant Needs and Solutions

| Need: | Provide: |
|---|---|
| **Physiological:** Includes oxygen, water, food, sex, and rest | Breaks, food, water, caffeine—and chocolate, if possible |
| **Safety and security:** Includes safe circumstances, stability, protection, and order | Safe environment, agenda, organization, security, lack of threats |
| **Social:** Includes need for love and belonging, friendships, and a sense of community | Group projects, opportunities for interaction, participant introductions |
| **Self-esteem:** The most basic is the need for the respect of others, the need for recognition, attention, reputation, appreciation, dignity, and even dominance. The higher form involves the need for self-respect, including such feelings as confidence, competence, achievement, mastery, independence, and freedom. | Recognize achievements, appreciate contributions, respect each individual, encourage, support, and provide opportunities for participants to share with each other and to succeed |

## McClelland's Theory of Learned Needs

David McClelland pioneered workplace motivational thinking with this theory, proposing that an individual's specific needs are acquired over time and are shaped by life experiences. This differs from Maslow's theory of needs that we have from birth. These learned needs are classed as achievement, affiliation, or power. A person's motivation and effectiveness in employment can be influenced by these three needs. McClelland's theory sometimes is referred to as the three-need theory, the learned needs theory, or the acquired-needs theory. It was used to improve employee assessment methods, advocating competency-based assessments and tests over traditional IQ and personality-based tests.

McClelland's theory includes the needs for:

- *Achievement* – People with a high need for achievement seek to excel and tend to avoid both low-risk and high-risk situations. Achievers avoid low-risk situations because an easily attained success is not a genuine achievement. In high-risk projects, achievers see the outcome as one of chance rather than one's own effort. These individuals prefer work that has a moderate probability of success, ideally a 50 percent chance. Achievers need regular feedback in order to monitor the progress of their achievements. They prefer either to work alone or with other high achievers, and like projects with reachable goals.

- *Affiliation* – Those with a high need for affiliation need harmonious relationships with other people and need to feel accepted by others. They tend to conform to the norms of their work group. These individuals prefer work that provides significant personal interaction. They perform well in customer service and client interaction situations, and like group work.

- *Power* – A person's need for power can be one of two types: personal and institutional. Those who need personal power want to direct others, and this need often is perceived as undesirable. People who need institutional power (also known as social power) want to organize the efforts of others to further the goals of the organization. Managers with a high need for institutional power tend to be more effective than those with a high need for personal power. In training, they will prefer to be the person in charge of a group.

For trainers, understanding what motivates these types of participants can be helpful in developing appropriate activities and exercises in workshops. It also helps in understanding how participants perform during group work.

## The ARCS Motivation Model

John Keller's ARCS Motivation Model is especially useful to keep in mind when planning and delivering training, so this model will be covered most thoroughly. Keller synthesized existing research on psychological motivation to create a theory with four major categories: **A**ttention, **R**elevance, **C**onfidence, and **S**atisfaction. His model is also based on social learning theories, which attest that motivation is dependent on human interactions. Keller is a professor of instructional systems and educational psychology at Florida State University, and his theory is compatible with traditional instructional systems design.

Keller acknowledges that both behavioral psychology and cognitive psychology have significant influence on instructional technology. Behavioral elements involve controlling outcomes with appropriate reinforcement. Cognitive elements concentrate on the analysis of content, the participants' prerequisite skills and abilities, and on how to organize and sequence content to best adapt to how participants process information. According to Keller, motivation involves both extrinsic and intrinsic factors. Each of his categories is further explained in the following sections.[1]

### Attention

- *Perceptual Arousal* – Gain and maintain attention by the use of novel, surprising, or uncertain events.

- *Inquiry Arousal* – Stimulate information-seeking behavior by asking or having the learner develop thought-provoking questions, a problem to solve, or brainstorming techniques.

- *Variability* – Maintain interest by adding variety to the workshop, such as exercises, videos, and guest speakers.

Start with something scintillating. Capture participants' interest with a "shocking" statistic. For example, how many people are on the Internet, or how many new Web sites are added every hour? There is an information hurricane! Or tell them three exciting things they will learn to do faster or better. Tell them what you like most about the software. Try to make it exciting. Think of the tactics of "get rich quick" speakers who advertise their programs with: "I'll tell you what the people in the financial industry (or real estate) don't want you to know ..." Tell people you will let them in on librarians' secrets!

Give a compelling, personally motivating reason or benefit for what you're teaching, before you teach it. Knowledge cannot be pushed into people's heads while they sit passively reading or listening; knowledge is co-creation. The participant must construct the new knowledge in his own head. For learners to be motivated, they must be engaged and involved.

To keep your students' attention, vary class pace and use different types of exercises. You can break up the workshop into 15-minute segments of mini-lectures, question-and-answer portions, practice exercises, group activities, and guided and independent work. This not only provides variability, but also accommodates the different learning styles discussed in Chapter 4.

If you are not excited about the topic, the participants will not be either. No one wants to sit through a boring, monotone lecture. Incorporate learning games, activities, or even a fun theme to raise learners' enthusiasm—and your own! Raise their curiosity levels with interesting examples or problems to solve.

### Relevance

- *Familiarity* – Use easy-to-understand language, examples, and concepts related to the learners' experience and values to help them integrate new information into their existing knowledge.

- *Goal Orientation* – Provide the learning objectives and how the technology is useful. Either give goals for the workshop or have the participants create their own.

- *Motive Matching* – Use training strategies that match the participants' motives.

# Survey Question: How Do You Create and Maintain Interest?

*Sarah Houghton-Jan, Information and Web Services Manager, San Mateo County Library, San Mateo (CA) –* "The best way to get students interested in training material is to mix the day up. Have them get up and move around, especially during computer training. Enforce some good ergonomics exercises as part of the training. Have them work individually, engage in group discussion, work in small groups, report back. All of that will keep them from getting the 'undergraduate lecture hall' glazed look."

*Max Anderson, Educational Services Librarian, SOLINET, Atlanta (GA) –* "To create and maintain interest in my classes, I tend to include a lot of exercises. I will do a brief demo, and then give the students an opportunity to practice what they just learned. I also like to use interesting examples when I am doing demos of search strategies—hopefully they are funny, and help wake them up! In a typical 9 AM to 4 PM face-to-face class, there is a 15-minute break in the morning, at least an hour lunch break and then another 15-minute break in the afternoon. I also use 'WebQuests,' which, according to Bernie Dodge, the originator of the WebQuest concept, are 'an inquiry-oriented activity in which most or all of the information used by learners is drawn from the Web. WebQuests are designed to use learners' time well, to focus on *using* information rather than on looking for it, and to support learners' thinking at the levels of analysis, synthesis, and evaluation.'"

Help participants see the relevance of the topic to their work, their interests, and their goals. Answer the WIIFM (What's in it for me?) questions. What are the benefits of the technology? How can it be useful to them? Will the training help them on their jobs, make their work easier, more effective, or efficient? How could the skills be used in their personal lives? Will this solve a problem they are having? Will it provide opportunities for them? Even better, let participants work on their own objectives. Have the class as a whole pick the learning objectives for the workshop. Give them a list of seven or eight options, and have them pick three or four to focus on. Write each objective on a flipchart and give them stickers to vote with.

When we're talking about true learning—especially recall and retention—the participants' goals are very important. Often, we assume that if they have taken the time to find, register, and possibly even pay for the training, they're obviously motivated. After all, they wouldn't be bothering if they weren't trying to learn something. Remember, though, that people are probably taking the technology workshop out of intrinsically motivated intellectual curiosity—because they need to do something. Anything not clearly relevant to that goal is just in the way. Appearance counts. It's not how relevant a particular topic is that matters—it's all about whether you have proven that to the participant, up front. And you have to keep on proving it over and over and over throughout the workshop.

Just saying that a topic is important is insufficient; this won't keep attendees' brains engaged, even if they trust you. You must demonstrate its importance before you expect them to pay attention and learn. If you wait until after you have explained something to give examples of why it matters or how participants can use it, it will probably be too late to matter to them.

Begin your workshop, then, by putting the technology in context. For example, if you are doing a workshop on blogs, don't start by going to Blogger.com and having people make one. First, show how blogs are relevant, how and why they should blog, and then show examples of current blogs, both professional and personal. Once they understand the big picture, you can show them how easy it is to make one of their own. In my workshop on blogs, I show the class the blog my husband made when we were remodeling our kitchen. Having a friendly example seems to break the ice and make the topic applicable.

Use stories and examples from real life experiences, which will help learners understand how they will apply what they learn to their own needs. The workshop must be relevant to each person's needs and interests, curiosity, and emotions, so relate the training to how they will be using it. Let them see the benefits by using examples that are applicable to their work or personal experience. The more personal a training experience, the more memorable it will be. Reality-based examples allow participants to see an immediate benefit. As Michael Porter, Community Associate, WebJunction, Seattle (WA) suggests: "Always use examples of other people, libraries, or library staff using what you are teaching in successful ways. People like to know what you are showing them is going to work. They especially like to know it is going to work after you have left and they aren't in class anymore."

Build learning on what people already know. Give them time to share their experiences, ask them about topic-related frustrations they have, and point out how the training will alleviate these. Sarah Houghton-Jan, Information and Web Services Manager, San Mateo County Library, San Mateo (CA), says: "Whatever topic you are training on, get the students to focus on something that they are interested in. Teaching basic Web searching? Have students search for something individually meaningful to them—not some boring example you have chosen. Teaching how to use RSS? Have students search for feeds on topics of interest to them. They will walk away having absorbed more and be more willing to try the technology after the class." Lastly, give them time for reflection to discover how what they've learned can be applicable to their own projects.

### Confidence

- *Expectancy for Success* – Make learners aware of what they will be doing in the workshop and how they will know if they are successful.

- *Challenge Setting Independence* – Allow learners to set personal goals or standards of accomplishment, and opportunities that allow them to experience success on their own.

- *Attribution Molding* – Give feedback and help participants build self-confidence.

Create opportunities for participants to build their confidence about the topic. They must see they are capable, that they can succeed in completing tasks themselves. Studies have shown that when adults are able to participate in learning and feel confident in their practice work, they retain more information and are better able to use it in their own lives.

Of course, patience is a virtue, especially with technology training. Participants get frustrated if they don't feel respected. Let them practice at their own pace. Use self-paced exercises so that both fast and experienced learners can work on their own. You are a guide; you are there to help participants achieve their own success. You can't learn for them.

Give them praise, encouragement, and approval. Share a funny experience you've had using or learning about the workshop topic; this will help participants relate to you and show them how you have overcome some of the same hurdles they may be facing. This will give them hope. For example, I tell my Emerging Technology participants that I got behind on the new technologies, and suddenly felt like I was 97 years old and had been living in a cabin without electricity. I then explain how I got caught up and how they can, too.

You can have people create a personalized action plan. This can be as simple as finishing the sentence, "I plan to … " Provide them with a handout that they can use during the workshop to write down what they want to learn and how they will apply it.

### Satisfaction

- *Natural Consequences and New Skills* – Provide opportunities to try newly acquired knowledge or skills in real-life situations.

- *Positive Consequences* – Provide feedback and support; let them know they can be successful.

- *Equity* – Maintain a fair and impartial objectivity.

Satisfaction can be gained in technology workshops by participants who are able to accomplish what they wanted to when they originally registered. Give them opportunities to work on their own and in groups and to test out their new skills themselves; they will gain the satisfaction of achieving their goals. Participants leaving your workshop should feel satisfied, whether through a sense of achievement or by having gained new skills that can be immediately useful. Use a review activity to make sure they remember what they've learned—and so that they realize how much they've learned.

Businesses are only successful if they have happy, satisfied customers. The same is true of a library. How can we help create more satisfied customers, who in turn are voters more likely to support libraries and their services? One way to do this is through our technology workshops.


## Using Examples and Analogies

An analogy is a comparison that creates a relationship between two dissimilar concepts. Analogies can help participants relate new information to their previous knowledge or experience. This makes learning easier, and increases retention by making abstract concepts concrete and real. One analogy that usually brings a smile is to compare opening a program to opening a door. Just like in a knock-knock joke—you always say "Knock, Knock," you never just say "Knock." Opening a program is just like opening a door, you always click twice. "Click, Click" is like "Knock, Knock, who's there!" Here are some favorite technology analogies from expert trainers:

*Meredith Farkas, Distance Learning Librarian, Norwich University, Northfield (VT)* – "This is what I often tell people when I'm teaching people about social software technologies: I don't know how the internal mechanisms of my car work, and yet I'm able to use it to get me where I need to go. It's the same with technologies. You usually don't need to know exactly how it works behind the scenes; you just need to know how to get it to do what you need it to do."

*Brenda Hough, Technology Coordinator, Northeast Kansas Library System, Lawrence (KS)* – "There's no denying that technology can be frustrating. I compare it to traffic. During a morning drive to work, for example, it's very likely that you will have something slightly frustrating occur (someone cuts you off, you miss a turn, etc.). Technology is like that, too. Things aren't always smooth and flawless. I often share this analogy near the beginning of class and then say that I expect there to be a few 'road bumps' during the class. I try to make it clear that this is just the nature of the beast, rather than the flaw of the individual. People who are new to technology are often so embarrassed or flustered when things go wrong. I try to set the stage, with those road bumps as an expectation. They are normal."

*Michael Porter, Community Associate, WebJunction, Seattle (WA)* – "I LOVE analogies, but I always make them up on the fly. Then I ask the class to critique the analogy and help me come up with another/better one. It's a fun exercise."

*Sarah Houghton-Jan, Information and Web Services Manager, San Mateo County Library, San Mateo (CA)* – "Learning technology is like learning how the human body works. The different parts all work together to make the entire organism work the way it does. You may not need to know how each mitochondrion works to know how your circulatory system works, but you do need to know the various types of cells and how the heart works, a related function. Technology is all interrelated, whether you're talking about how the interface to the new Windows OS works or the way your digital camera uploads photos. Skills from one area are transferable to another, and they all connect."

*Erin James, Library Associate, Gwinnett County Public Library, Lilburn (GA)* – "I've tried to explain my blog aggregator (first Bloglines, now Google Reader) to some co-workers. What finally seemed to stick was: This is like my personal newspaper—I decide what types of news show up, and I only get the freshest news delivered. And, it never lands in the bushes!

*Anonymous* – "A feed reader is to RSS like a Web browser is to HTML."

*Mindy Johnson, Head of Adult Services, Camden County Library, Voorhees (NJ)* – "I tell newcomers to the mouse to move it around like 'an iron on a delicate shirt.' Also, when showing them not to click until they are on the link; saying 'think of how you don't put a car in park until you're stopped' helps. For double-clicking, we'll ask if they remember the Little Caesar's 'pizza pizza' commercial … that's the speed they want."

*Chris Peters, Information Technology Specialist, Washington State Library, Olympia (WA)* –"The Web before RSS was like the days before printing. You had to travel from place to place to get news and information. With RSS, the news shows up on your doorstep every morning. What's even better is, you're getting a newspaper that's customized to your tastes and interests."

*Anonymous* – "I use a lot of analogies to relate computers to 'real world' counterparts. I describe files and folders in relation to a filing cabinet. The operating system desktop is just like your desk with papers (shortcuts) to things you are working on, and tools you use regularly."

## A Learning Climate

The physical environment always comes into play. First, consider the basics that relate to human needs such as temperature, food, water, restrooms, chairs, lighting, and acoustics. Other factors, though, can also affect learning. Make sure the training room is as clean and organized as possible. Tell participants to make themselves comfortable. Mention that they can adjust the screen angle, the mouse placement, and the chairs (especially ergonomic chairs). Let them know they are free to use the facilities when they need to.

Another factor is actually color. Psychologists report that bright colors tend to be more conducive to learning than dark, dull colors. And what color are most library computer labs? White? What color are computers? Black, putty, beige? If you can, at least paint the room. If not, there are some easy and less expensive things you can do. Use flipchart paper, construction paper, and posters. Use a theme and hang mobiles from the ceiling. Go to a party store and buy some big colored plastic or paper tablecloths. Color can make a big difference.

Kinesthetic learners love manipulatives, toys, and things they can do with their hands. If participants won't be on the computer the entire workshop, consider having pipe cleaners, stress balls, or small toys they can use creatively. Incentives are always wildly appreciated as well, even inexpensive toys and candy. See Chapter 11 for sources of cheap yet fun incentives.

Develop an open, friendly, and low-stress atmosphere. Encourage participants to learn and explore. Let them know it is always all right to ask questions and try things out for themselves. Encourage questions and discussions.

Make a point of showcasing other library resources and services that relate to the workshop topic. This is very useful, both to give participants concrete examples and to build awareness of the library's offerings. You can bring along print and electronic media materials, introduce databases, and discuss reference services. Use the opportunity for a quick commercial for the library. Many people won't know about everything your library offers for free.

Of course, along with this friendly, self-help atmosphere, participants also need order and respect. Many trainers find some ground rules to be helpful. These rules can even be quickly determined as a group at the beginning of the workshop. Let them name a few and go with those. Usually the group will come up with things that you'll appreciate as well, such as treating each other with respect, putting cell phones on vibrate, not having side discussions, getting back from breaks on time, and signaling when discussions go off-topic. Record these on a whiteboard or flipchart so everyone can see them.

## Subject Specific Classes

When providing introductory Internet or other basic classes, trainers can easily become bored by having to train on the same material again and again. Re-energize yourself by, for instance,

Table 6.2   Ideas for Subject Specific Classes

| | | | |
|---|---|---|---|
| Travel Planning (partner with travel agency) | Gardening (partner with gardening clubs, garden centers, parks) | Making a Scrapbook (partner with craft shops) | eBay (partner with high-sellers, collectors) |
| Job Searching on the Internet (partner with local workforce center, job hunters, employment agencies) | Recipes (partner with cooking schools, restaurants) | Antiques (partner with appraisers, antique stores) | Welcome to the Neighborhood (partner with Chamber of Commerce, Welcome Wagon, neighborhood association) |
| E-mail for Seniors (partner with teens, senior groups, retirement centers) | Health Information on the Web (partner with health clinics, medical libraries) | Genealogy 101 (partner with genealogy society, local historical museum) | Surfing for Kids (partner with teachers, parent groups, local Internet Service Provider) |
| Day Trips in Your Backyard (partner with B&Bs, resorts, national parks) | Retirement Resources on the Web (partner with financial planners, AARP, clubs) | Health and Fitness (partner with nutritionists, gyms, personal trainers) | Internet for Seniors (partner with high school students, volunteer organizations such as the Senior Corps) |
| Buying a House/Car/Computer (partner with real estate agents, automobile clubs, computer clubs) | Wedding Planning (partner with wedding planners, wedding shops, resorts) | Pregnancy (partner with health clinics, doulas, baby stores, pediatricians, hospitals) | Ceramics (partner with local artists, art centers, colleges) |

focusing on different subject specific information on the Internet. You don't even need to be a subject matter expert; you can bring in an expert to deliver that part of the class. These classes also allow you to focus and not feel like your information is so broad that your patrons can't relate to it. Just as academic reference librarians design presentations for specific classes, addressing research tools and techniques needed for a specific topic or assignment, think of what you most enjoy using the technology for, and try to work interesting topics into your basic workshops.

One anonymous survey respondent shares: "I have experience in genealogy, so I offer a couple of genealogy classes. The other instructor is experienced in selling on eBay, so she offers classes on eBay. We also work with homeschoolers to offer Workplace Skills so that they can be eligible for a Hiring Certificate for employment. This is a grant program that was funded to offer the homeschoolers the same type of program that is taught in the public schools."

While working at the Bill & Melinda Gates Foundation, trainer (and then co-worker) Brenda Hough and I developed a workshop for state libraries and large public library systems titled "Nothin' But Net: How to Score Big with Internet Training." Some of the information from this workshop is now available on WebJunction (webjunction.org/do/DisplayContent;jsessionid=17D756A87795B 01FE122F0158F0E4CD9?id=1374), and Table 6.2 includes some of the ideas that we generated on example workshops. I've also included ideas for partners, but I'm sure you can think of even more! Chapter 10 lists additional examples.

## Endnotes

1. John M. Keller and Katsuaki Suzuki, "Application of the ARCS model to courseware design," *Instructional Designs for Microcomputer Courseware*, ed. David H. Jonassen, Hillsdale, NJ. L. Erlbaum Associates, 1988: 401–434.

## Chapter 7

# Planning Technology Training

*If you want one year of prosperity—grow grain. If you want ten years of prosperity—grow trees. If you want one hundred years of prosperity—grow people.*

—Chinese Proverb

Although you may have fallen into your training responsibilities accidentally, good planning is no accident. Examine the purpose and type of technology training needed at your library to help you gain insight into the planning and resources necessary. Use the library's vision and strategic plan as the foundation for technology training plans. Determine training goals for the library that support the greater mission and that integrate technology training into existing library programs. This chapter focuses on planning your overall training program, while Chapter 8 covers planning for individual workshop sessions.

Planning must occur whether training is to be held as formal classes or just as one-on-one, on-the-fly training when the public asks questions. Because many accidental library trainers are juggling training responsibilities and other job tasks, such as reference work or technology support, planning helps you balance your duties. As the Buddhist saying goes: "We have very little time, therefore, we must proceed very slowly." Planning will help you save time and develop priorities.

## Training and Development Plan

Every library should develop some sort of training and development plan, even if offering only informal public and/or staff training. Sketching out a plan with goals, intended methods, and outcomes will at least give you a sense of what you want and of how you'll know if you've been successful. Don't expect perfection, either in the plan or in its implementation. Just start simple, and then update it as you go along. There is no perfect plan; yours just needs to meet the needs of your individual library, your staff, and your community members.

If you are at a small library—or even if you are at a large system, but far down on the totem pole—don't let the thought of planning overwhelm you. Think of it as strategizing. Spend just one hour focusing on the elements in your training plan. Then, ask another staff member to brainstorm with you and see what develops. Libraries need both a staff and a public training plan, because the participants and their needs are very different. Some basic elements of training plans include:

1. Training Mission/Purpose Statement
2. Needs Assessment
3. Goals and Objectives
4. Methodology and Resources
5. Outcomes and Evaluation
6. Policies and Procedures

You should begin by examining your library's mission and strategic plan (if it has one). These will help guide the purpose behind the training program. Also, look at any recent community planning that may have been done to see whether the library can use technology training to meet goals already established by your community. This can be a great opportunity to fulfill real needs.

Training is also often included as part of the activities of a strategic plan—as part of the actions that are planned to achieve the goals and objectives. A training plan should include a list of who should get trained and on what, a budget for training, and a schedule for training.

One widely used method for developing training programs is Instructional Systems Design (ISD). There are many different models, but most are based on five steps represented by the acronym ADDIE. These steps are: Analysis (performing a needs assessment and setting goals); Design (determining content and delivery methods); Development (creating lesson plans and materials); Implementation (conduct the training); and Evaluation (examining results).

During analysis, the designer develops a clear understanding of the "gaps" between the desired outcomes or behaviors and the audience's existing knowledge and skills. The design phase documents specific learning objectives, assessment instruments, exercises, and content. The actual creation of learning materials is completed in the development phase. During implementation, these materials are delivered or distributed to the student group. After delivery, the effectiveness of the training materials is evaluated.

### Training Mission/Purpose Statement

The mission or purpose statement for your technology training program outlines the reasons why your library determined it should offer technology training for staff and/or the public. It answers the simple question: Why are you providing technology workshops? An example of a training purpose statement is: "The library supplies various software programs and Internet access to further our mission of providing informational and educational resources to our community. The library provides training and instruction on how to use technology resources and assistance in lifelong learning skills as part of its service responses to community needs."

## Staff Training Plans

It is important to develop a staff technology training plan. Technology isn't worth anything unless people are using it, and training staff enables them to make the most out of the library's technology investments. Developing a staff training plan helps you evaluate what training staff members need, so you can budget for training materials and classes, prioritize training on specific technology for specific people, and investigate ways to stretch your training dollars.

Encourage staff to develop their own individual learning plans, in which they set their own goals and identify for themselves the areas they need to learn more about. Your training plan can also include in-house training, where employees who have learned about an application or technology can train others. For example, if you send one employee to a class, that employee can pass his or her new skills on to others. Have staff complete a "Transfer of Learning" form where they describe how they will use their knowledge in their jobs, and how they will continue their learning. (Find a sample transfer of learning form on the Minnesota Voluntary Certification for Library Employees site, www.arrowhead.lib.mn. us/certification/transfer.htm.)

In a staff training plan, you should ideally determine the minimum level of technology competency required for each staff position. This lets you assess each person's proficiency with the technology they need to use. The training plan can include workshops or classes, independent learning materials (such as online resources, books, CDs, or videotapes), and time for practice and proficiency. Remember to include training in your annual budget and in appropriate grant proposals.

Of course, you may discover that all the library staff members need training, but your budget is $0. If so, look at Chapter 10 for one possible solution in the Public Library of Charlotte & Mecklenburg County's Learning 2.0 Program. This program involved letting staff learn on their own about social networking tools, but could also be applied to other technology topics.

TechAtlas (techatlas.org), a Web-based technology management and planning tool provided free of charge through WebJunction, helps libraries inventory their technology assets and use that information as a starting point for building a comprehensive technology plan. One of these assets is library staff. One area in TechAtlas, the "Staff Professional Development Assessment," helps libraries assess staff training programs. The questions it asks include:

1. *Evaluating current professional development activities* – Make sure that staff professional development is fully integrated into your library's vision and mission:

   - Does your library provide recognition for staff members who attend training or otherwise achieve learning goals?

   - Does your library integrate professional development goals into the performance evaluation process for your staff members?

   - Does your library have in-house "technology gurus" who offer training to other staff members?

2. *Recognizing barriers to professional development* – Identify and challenge obstacles to your staff professional development program:

   - Does your library expect staff members to attend training outside of regular working hours?

   - Does your library have a procedure in place for staff to request training?

- Do you have a current record of staff members' preferred learning styles?

3. *Determining professional development needs* – Make sure that your staff development program is producing the results your library needs:

   - Do you have a current record of staff members' computer skills?

   - Do all staff members receive sufficient training to satisfy technology core competencies for their jobs?

   - Do you have an evaluation process in place to gather feedback on training from staff?

4. *Maintaining a professional development culture* – Keep your staff development program going with resources for individual learning:

   - Does your library encourage staff members to share what they have learned with their peers after participating in training events?

   - Do you communicate information about available training opportunities to all members of the library staff?

   - Does your library offer a variety of training options (self-paced books, online courses and tools, classroom training, and peer learning) for staff to choose from?

5. *Funding professional development* – Ensure that you are budgeting sufficient funds to meet your staff development goals and objectives:

   - Does your library include funds for staff technology training in grant proposals and other financial support requests?

   - Which statement best describes your library's training budget?

- Can you partner with other libraries or nonprofit organizations in your community to pursue shared training opportunities (and share costs)?

After completing the TechAtlas training assessment, a library receives a list of recommendations for helping staff strengthen their technology skills. These may include:

- Develop a staff technology training plan

- Plan for the design and delivery of training

- Make the library a learning organization by supporting ongoing and peer learning

- Notify all library staff members of training opportunities as they become available

- Develop competencies and learning goals based on each staff member's role

- Assess staff members' technology skills in order to identify training needs

- Design and communicate a clear procedure for staff to request training

- Make staff technology training a mandatory part of your funding requests and your library budget

- Have library staff members self-assess their learning style preferences

- Support multiple learning styles to increase staff learning success

- Recruit trainers from your own staff—ask in-house experts to share their knowledge

- Build professional development goals into the staff performance evaluation process

- Develop a procedure for evaluating the success of training

- Provide recognition for library staff members who achieve learning goals

## Needs Assessment

A needs assessment determines the topics on which you will need to provide training. What training needs to be done to get your library and community members the skills and knowledge they want? What will help the library achieve its goals and support its mission?

There are many ways to conduct a needs assessment. You can conduct interviews with a few key community leaders, facilitate some focus groups, administer questionnaires, and/or observe and track requests for information. Tracking and analyzing questions that the public regularly asks can help determine useful topics. You could also notice what types of books are being checked out or what current topics are discussed on radio talk shows on stations like National Public Radio. Another source of information could be popular stories in the local newspaper or on the television news.

Look at what is going on your community. Do people need help completing online job applications? Do older adults have questions about getting online? Do students need help with online research? Do teens need activities and a safe place to be after school?

Beyond just basic technology skills, think about what people need to know to keep up with new technologies. The report *Confronting the Challenges of Participatory Culture: Media Education for the 21st Century,* mentioned in Chapter 1, includes cultural competencies and social skills as new media literacies that are developed through collaboration and networking in online communities.

*Competencies*

For your staff training program, you should use core technology competencies to help determine the skills needed. Competencies are areas of capability that allow people to perform successfully in their jobs by completing tasks effectively. A competency can be knowledge, attitudes, skills, or personal values; competencies can be acquired through experience or training. A number of examples of library technology competencies have been developed. You could adapt one of these for your staff, or, if your state has a library certification process, use the competencies associated with that program. Examples of library technology competencies include:

- *California Library Association Technology Core Competencies for CA Library Workers* (www.cla-net.org/included/docs/tech_core_competencies.pdf)

- The Public Library Association's *Technology for Results: Developing Service-Based Plans* (Chicago: ALA, 2005) includes a "Technical Skills Assessment"

- *Western Council Core Competencies* (westernco.org/continuum/LCPPfinal.pdf) developed by the Western Council of State Libraries, includes a technology competency

Once you outline a list of competencies, you need to assess library staff to find out whether they already have these skills or if they require additional training. You could use an online survey, developed in-house using a tool like Zoomerang (zoomerang.com) or SurveyMonkey (surveymonkey.com). You could also use TechAtlas, which provides free online surveys to help evaluate staff training needs. The person who manages/creates the survey can e-mail a link to a list of recipients, and then monitor how many have responded. They don't need to be registered TechAtlas users to take the survey; they just need a Web browser.

TechAtlas keeps track of who has submitted the survey and can even send out reminders to people who haven't responded, while results can be displayed in graph format or exported as Excel data. Its recommendations for training are general and based on how high an individual scores in each area.  TechAtlas surveys cover a variety of basic technology competencies, including things most staff members will need to know, such as word processing skills, Internet skills, e-mail skills, and troubleshooting skills. People are able to rank their comfort level with the different skills in each section.

### Target Audiences

Planning for public workshops involves determining target audiences. The specific needs of each audience must be considered when deciding what type of training needs to be conducted. Of course, a workshop topic could often be relevant to several different groups. Examples of groups you might want to serve by developing specialized technology workshops include:

- Older adults
- Boomers
- Job seekers
- Businesspersons
- New immigrants
- Teens
- Winter visitors
- Nonprofit organizations
- Tourists
- Teachers
- Children

- College students

- Parents

- Twenty-somethings

- Adults new to technology

- At-home business owners

- Spanish speakers

### *Appreciative Inquiry*

Appreciative Inquiry is used by the business world to build on successes instead of dwelling on problems. You can use this technique to examine what works well in your library. Are some workshops more popular than others? Maybe you should offer more of those types, or find out why they are popular—is it the content or the trainer? What library services are in high demand?

I was talking to a group of rural librarians who were complaining about how teens love to crowd around a single computer to share what they are doing—looking at MySpace, playing a game, etc. These librarians felt it was disruptive. One even said that she has had to reprimand families as well—that sometimes parents and children were trying to use one computer. You can turn this around and think of these types of situations as opportunities, rather than problems to be avoided. Using appreciative inquiry, you could view this behavior as a success to be built on.

If using a computer socially is in demand, why would we take so much staff time to keep it from happening? We are being the shushing librarians again! Why not set up some computers specifically for this type of use, perhaps set aside a few shared computers in the teen room? If your library is smaller and doesn't have room for extra computers, consider designating a specific hour of the day for shared computer use, or looking for funding to expand your technology space. Parker Public Library in Parker, Arizona, is a very small rural library that wrote grants to build a room onto its library. In 2004, the Parker Public Library opened its 1,000-square-foot Lifelong Learning Center. The Arizona Department of Housing awarded the library a Community Block Grant of $127,500 for construction, and the Arizona State Library gave $20,000 for laptop computers, furnishings, and materials for technology workshops. The Friends of the Parker Public Library donated $3,500 toward two study rooms. They have computers in these rooms, as well as their teen room (that was designed from the reconfigured space), and also provide wireless access so community members can bring in their own laptops and participate in technology workshops. In the new rooms, some small study rooms were added that can also be used for shared computer use.

In many of our communities, free computer use is only possible in the library. So why not make this an area in which we excel? Look at what the public wants and how people are using the technology in a social sense. Focus on making that something we are known for, instead of being known for our rules and admonishments.

### Goals and Objectives

Establishing clear goals and objectives involves figuring out what you want to accomplish and the strategies you will use to get the results you want. Your goals and objectives correspond directly to the evaluation of your training program in that they form the standards that will be measured. Goals are broad, general statements that describe what you are working toward, what the outcome will be. Goals are the path to achieving the training mission and the solution to fulfilling the needs identified in the needs assessments.

Some goals may be short-term while others could cover a multi-year period. All goals should be written in positive language, as if they have already occurred. Examine your existing library plan and use it as a guide to determine what the training program should be working toward. For example, one of the library's strategic goals could be: "Make community members aware of the importance and purpose of the library's resources and services." Think about how technology training can help fulfill this intention. Some ideas include the following goals: "City and county government employees attend technology workshops available through the library on programs and resources that benefit them in doing their jobs" or "Teens have access to and understand how to use online library resources and support for their educational needs."

Objectives are written for each goal, but may also relate to more than one goal. Objectives are short-range and more focused than goals. These are how a library can measure its progress toward reaching a goal, so it must be very clear what the objective will accomplish and how it will be measured. The acronym SMART, which stands for **S**pecific, **M**easurable, **A**chievable, **R**ealistic, and **T**ime-bound, is often used as a way to remember the important elements in writing objectives. As you write objectives, keep these criteria in mind; check each objective to see if it meets these conditions.

An easy formula for writing objectives includes:

1. A specific, realistic, and achievable end result (for example, "to increase the number of teens that attend technology workshops")

2. The unit of measurement (for example, "40 percent")

3. The date the objective will be accomplished (for example, "by January 2009")

When you combine these three elements, your objective becomes: "By January 2009, the number of teens who attend technology workshops in a given year will increase by 40 percent." Another example is: "90 percent of participants who take library technology training workshops will demonstrate new skills and will rate on an evaluation form that they were very satisfied with the program in 2009."

An excellent planning process for libraries is Sandra S. Nelson's *The New Planning for Results: A Streamlined Approach* (Chicago: PLA, 2001). If implemented correctly, this is a wonderful way to incorporate community input into your planning process; it has been used successfully by all types of libraries, not just public.

The model includes a set of service responses that are used for setting service and program priorities based on community needs. In 2007, the PLA is updating these service responses to better reflect the changes that have occurred in traditional library work. By examining the draft version of these new roles (www.plaresults. org/service_response_links.htm), it is evident that each one can be accomplished through technology training. If your library doesn't have a strategic plan, it can be helpful to use these service responses as a guide to prioritize your library's roles. (No library, though, should be offering every one of these services; we cannot be everything to everyone, no matter how much we might want to be.) Select three to four of these to help focus your training offerings, based on your community's needs:

Be Informed Citizens: Local, National, and World Affairs

Build Successful Enterprises: Business and Nonprofit Support

Connect to the Online World: Public Internet Access

Create Young Readers: Emergent Literacy

Discover Your Heritage: Genealogy and Local History

Explore Our Community: Community Resources and Services

Express Creativity: Create and Share Content

Get Fast Facts: Ready Reference

Know How to Find, Evaluate, and Use Information: Information Fluency

Learn to Read and Write: Adult, Teen, and Family Literacy

Make Career Choices: Job and Career Development

Make Informed Decisions: Health, Wealth, and Other Life Choices

Satisfy Curiosity: Lifelong Learning

Stimulate Imagination: Reading, Viewing, and Listening for Pleasure

Succeed in School: Homework Help

Visit a Comfortable Place: Public and Virtual Spaces

Welcome to the United States: Services for New Immigrants

## Methodology and Resources

Library technology workshops are the activities that will accomplish your training goals and objectives. Training does require quite a few resources, from identifying the specific people who will be involved with training at the library to examining the training space and setup, whether in a computer lab or on the library floor.

### Trainers

Since you are reading this book, you may have already been selected as your library technology trainer. If possible, though, it is always advisable to try to have someone help you with your technology workshops. Having an assistant available when there are technical problems, slow learners, or just to lend a hand to get everything set up can be a big help in making your workshops more successful.

A training team or committee can also be very useful. Following, find some of the skills team members should have (not that each person must have all the skills), and some of the responsibilities that can be shared:

*Training Team Skills and Abilities.*
* Understanding of the interests and needs of participants

- Experts in knowledge/learning

- Connectors, they know people

- Interest in training issues

- Willingness to serve and participate

- Availability

- Work well in a group

- Writing skills

- Access to administration

*Training Team Responsibilities:*
- Managing entire training program

- Designing individual workshops

- Identifying trainers

- Creating training schedules

- Identifying target audiences

- Conducting training needs assessment

- Budgeting of training program

- Ongoing communication with trainers

- Coordinating publicity, within each library and community

- Handling registrations

- Meeting speakers

- Introducing trainers

- Reserving meeting room/computer labs

- Offering technology support

- Training assistance

- Making handout copies

- Arranging room

- Greeting participants

- Buying refreshments and setting up

- Writing thank-you notes

- Compiling evaluations

- Reporting on workshops to administration

### Volunteers

Beyond just using library staff as trainers, look outside your four walls and find assistance in your community. You can use volunteers to be the primary trainer or an assistant trainer, create handouts and lesson plans, develop marketing materials, call or e-mail reminders to participants, or even create online tutorials. They could monitor the computer lab during open hours and assist with basic technology questions. Many schools are requiring a community service requirement, so teens may be looking for an opportunity like this.

*Possible volunteer trainers include:*
- Seniors (seniornet.org can be helpful)

- High school students/teen volunteers

- Regional systems

- State library staff

- Community recreation departments

- Continuing education departments

- Literacy councils

- Community college students

- Interns from a university

- Vocational/technical college students

- Local business people

- Electronics/computer vendors

- Computer clubs

- City technology staff

- Parents

- Volunteer organizations

- Teachers

- Retired teachers or librarians

- Professional instructors

- Current volunteers

- Other local libraries (trade trainers and topics!)

Some librarians are hesitant when it comes to volunteers in their library; I have heard horror stories that have resulted in libraries no longer using volunteers at all. However, many libraries find great success and are able to add services through the use of volunteers, and some are even operated completely by volunteers. One commonality among libraries that succeed in using volunteers is that they treat volunteers very much like staff members. This includes having a formal hiring process, encouraging involvement, giving advanced responsibilities (not just filing or shelving), and providing training, supervision, and some form of appreciation.

A great description of library volunteers is found on the Fond du Lac Public Library, Wisconsin Web site (www.fdlpl.org/volunteer. html):

> Volunteers bring the library enthusiasm, energy, added talents, and a fresh perspective. They enhance, rather than replace adequate staffing. They enrich the library's

offerings, rather than provide basic service. Volunteer service aids the library in making the best use of its fiscal resources and contributes to sound working relationships with other city departments, as well as with community groups and organizations. Volunteers are liaisons to the community and by their contribution are advocates for quality library service. The library and its volunteers work together for mutual satisfaction.

You should have volunteers complete an application form, and be sure to interview them. Perform a criminal background check on all volunteers, and instigate a probation period so that you can "try each other out." Make sure you have some requirements and stipulations, such as permission forms for volunteers under age 18, a letter of agreement outlining all responsibilities, and an understanding that they must follow all library rules and policies.

The library has a responsibility to provide volunteers with training, supervision, and recognition. Volunteers need supervision and someone to coordinate scheduling. This supervision could come from a part-time staff person or even a very trusted volunteer who has been involved with the library and demonstrated their competence. Make sure you also provide training on library policies and philosophies.

Try to offer volunteers some type of reward, such as free membership in the Friends of the Library, a special pre-shopping day before the annual book sale, waiving the first $5 of any library fines, longer circulation times (or no due dates at all), or a special T-shirt. Community recognition is a good reward as well. Publish their names in the newspaper or on a special wall in the library; throw them a party and send periodic thank-you letters.

Multnomah County Library in Oregon advertises for volunteers on the Volunteer Match Web site (www.volunteermatch.org). See

Chapter 10 for information on innovative teen technology volunteer programs, including Chicago Public Library's Cyber Navigators, Brooklyn Public Library's Technology Institute, and in-depth tips from Reading (MA) Public Library's Netguides Program.

### Training Space and Equipment

*Where will you offer training?*

- Computer lab

- Individual workstations

- Laptop labs

- Online, through tutorials, Webinars, Web sites, online courseware

- Collaboration rooms

- Community centers

- School labs

- On participants' laptops, if you have wireless access

### Types of Training

What form of training will your library offer? Learning in the library doesn't always take place in a classroom or formal setting. Learning may be as simple as answering a few questions and sharing a few tips. Libraries should plan to create spaces and opportunities for people to learn beyond meeting rooms. Think about how you could use technology discussion groups or technology sharing sessions. In *Developing Employees Who Love to Learn*, Linda Honold explains that: "Learning may take place through silent reflection, listening and synthesizing, hands-on application, or active experimentation."[1]

Here are some ideas, many gathered from WebJunction (web junction.org) members, for when training can take place. Offering training in a variety of forms and times is best, if you have the resources.

*When will you offer training?*
- Evenings

- After school

- When the library is closed

- Daytime

- Lunchtime

- 30-minute sessions

- On-the-fly, just when questions are asked

- Appointment based, one-on-one

- JITT: Just-in-Time Training; short sessions when needed


### Delivery Methods

The most common delivery method is the traditional technology workshop, typically offered as a one- to three-hour class. (See Chapter 10 for many ideas of workshops offered by libraries across the country.) Beyond traditional technology workshops, here are some other methods for delivering training—again, many suggested by WebJunction members:

- Form "learning partners"—teen/senior, senior/senior, staff/teen, staff/staff, etc.
- Coordinate training with other libraries
- Create online tutorials
- Record podcasts
- Create a learning blog
- Develop a staff wiki to share knowledge

- Share PowerPoint presentations

- Create Quick Guides (or download existing online ones)

- Provide a bibliography with "how to" books and Web sites

- Use in-person discussion groups

- Create an online discussion list

- Share a Web site or database of the week with everyone on staff or with the public

- Borrow a mobile computer lab from the state library, a regional system, or other local organization

- Make a descriptive list of databases, without library lingo

- Develop a staff-only Web site for staff notes and scheduling

- Use contests or learning games as motivators

## Outcomes and Evaluation

The first step in evaluating a training program is to examine the desired outcomes specified in the goals and objectives. With objectives defined, the measurement and metrics can be established to determine if the training had the desired effect. All of this can sound very time consuming until you apply it realistically. Typically, training is offered as a method for change. If the change happened, then the training was effective.

Evaluation can take many forms, including testing, assessments, and self-reflection. Some of these forms evaluate just the trainer, some just the participant, and some both. The six major reasons for evaluating training include:

- Improving the quality of the training (trainer)

- Promoting individual growth through self-evaluation (trainer and participant)

- Assessing demonstrated achievement; changes in skills, knowledge, behavior (participant)

- Determining future learning needs (trainer and participant)

- Enhancing personal sense of satisfaction and worth (trainer and participant)

- Proving whether the service is of value (trainer and participant, and especially the library)

Donald Kirkpatrick identified the evaluation model most widely recognized today in corporate training organizations. The Kirkpatrick Evaluation Model addresses the four fundamental behavior changes that occur as a result of training in an Evaluation Hierarchy. The four levels of the Kirkpatrick Evaluation Model are:

- *Level One—Reaction* measures how participants feel about training. This level is often measured with questionnaires that measure attitude. Sometimes called smile sheets, these evaluations answer the question, "Did you like it/me?"

- *Level Two—Learning* determines if people learned the material, even if just by memorization. This is often accomplished with pre-testing and post-testing.

- *Level Three—Behavior Change* answers the question, "Do people apply what they've learned?" This level addresses transference of new skills and is often accomplished by observation.

- *Level Four—Results* measures the training effectiveness, "What result has the training achieved?" This broad category is concerned with the impact of the program on the wider community.

The easiest way to evaluate on level one or two is through a simple evaluation form given out at the end of a workshop (one example is provided in Chapter 8). While level three can be accomplished by observing a participant completing hands-on work, it really may be hard to determine behavior change unless the individual is in a series of workshops, or unless you can follow up with them after the workshop. Level four can take more time and resources to accomplish, but this doesn't mean it should never happen.

These higher levels of evaluation really relate to Outcome Based Evaluation (OBE). Now, I know that those three letters can cause fear in a trainer. I admit that, when I first did training, I didn't really understand OBE—except that it was going to mean more work to compile information or submit detailed reports. A common definition for OBE is measuring the change in a person's behavior, skill, knowledge, attitude, or life condition.

This measurement is really a measurement of what someone *does* differently as a result of the training, which is best shown as a change in performance. It means that your learning objectives should focus on what a person can do for themselves as a result of the training. Beyond the ability to follow step-by-step instructions when they are reading your handout, OBE involves a person's ability to think through a situation on their own to find a solution.

This type of evaluation requires that you collect different information than that generally collected for traditional library statistics. For example, quantitative measurements assess outputs such as the number of people trained and the number of training hours delivered. This is relatively easy information to gather. Qualitative outcomes, including outcome-based evaluation, focus on whether participants learned what they needed to learn, whether behaviors were changed, whether they learned new skills, and whether they took on greater responsibility.

It is more difficult to conduct this type of assessment, but it provides a better indicator of whether your training program is really making an impact and is worth the resources the library is devoting.

Qualitative evaluation also provides the library with anecdotes that illustrate the effects of its programs and services. These descriptive narratives can be helpful in proving the library's value to administrators, local officials, fiscal entities, grantors, and others.

Let's look at the earlier sample objectives and see how they would be measured. The first one is: "By January 2009, the number of teens who attend technology workshops in a given year will increase by 40 percent." To measure this objective, you first need to know how many teens attended technology workshops in 2007, and also how many attended in 2008, so you can calculate whether the total for the year increased by 40 percent.

The second objective is: "90 percent of participants who take library technology training workshops will demonstrate new skills and will rate on an evaluation form that they were very satisfied with the program in 2009." To measure this objective, you will need to create an evaluation form that measures satisfaction levels and distribute it in every library technology workshop. You will also have to measure how the participants demonstrate new skills. You could have a trainer observe the participants completing tasks at the beginning and end of a workshop, or you could have participants take some type of assessment before the workshop, and follow up afterward.

As this demonstrates, your evaluation process has to be identified before you begin implementing any training program that you want to evaluate. You cannot know if training has helped the library progress toward a goal, toward a desired outcome, without first determining a starting point or a baseline against which you will measure.

If the training program is not immediately successful, don't automatically jump to conclusions as to why. I've seen some libraries determine that lack of success was due to the topic, when it might be the time of day or the month the workshop was offered, not enough publicity, lack of childcare, or any number of other reasons. The only person who can really know if someone learned something is the learner himself. And what if the learner already knew the content before he attended the workshop? In this case, he may write on an evaluation form that he did not learn anything new. That doesn't mean the workshop was not a success, it just means that it did not offer what that individual needed. If training goals are not accomplished, this is not an automatic failure; it indicates that a review should occur and that changes might be needed for success.

## Policies and Procedures

The policies and procedures needed for library training programs will vary from library to library. Policies are broad, written statements that assist in guiding actions and decisions that support library operations. Policies are not detailed courses of action; they are just explanations as to why a library does something. Procedures are created to support, implement, and give guidance and instructions to anyone involved with the policies.

Always put your policies and procedures in writing and make them available to staff and the public. They are necessary and helpful in supporting the library's mission, helping staff, board, and volunteers know how to do their jobs, and letting the community know what to expect from the library.

Policies and procedures you may need for training include those that detail how the library:

- Handles training registration, any fees, and cancellation arrangements

- Manages the computer lab and/or equipment

- Approves and manages staff training

- Selects topics for training

- Performs evaluation of trainers and of the training program

## Marketing the Workshops

Marketing and training have something important in common: Both aim to change a person's behavior, and both aim to establish credibility. While marketing may address the behavior of going to a store and buying a product, or being persuaded to believe in a service, training is also a type of persuasive activity. A trainer is attempting to facilitate a change in behavior, knowledge, skill, or attitude. You start by getting a person's attention and attracting them to the training you offer. Creating interest through promotion, marketing, and design is crucial to training success.

You know the saying, "If you build it, they will come." If only it were really that easy! I learned one of the most important lessons of my training career in conjunction with an event I planned while in library school. As ALA Student Chapter President, I decided one of my goals would be to coordinate a big community-wide event: A Read Aloud for the children. I contacted local celebrities to read their favorite children's story at an evening program, including a popular university football player, a local radio station host, and other prominent public figures. I was able to book the beautiful outdoor arena at the World's Fair site for no fee. I asked a local candy store to donate homemade candy and got a huge cake from a bakery. Yes, I was good at getting donations of space, celebrity readers, and food. But, unfortunately, my event was not a success, not at all.

On the night of the event, there were only a few people in the audience—and only two were children, who were brought by one of my classmates. The press came, and I was interviewed for the evening news. Somehow, thankfully, the cameraman managed to take a shot of the two kids, zoomed in so it looked like they were just two of many happy children eating free candy and spellbound by the show (the football player did an amazing job!). They didn't show the huge auditorium with hundreds of empty seats. And, thankfully, they didn't make my big mistake known to the public. It must have been a slow news night in Knoxville, Tennessee!

I learned a few important things from this. I should have worked for buy-in from all my colleagues and the support of the faculty members. I should have assigned an entire sub-committee to advertise and market instead of delegating that very important responsibility to one person. And I shouldn't have focused on the celebrity readers and the event at the expense of the audience. At least the news story that aired was aimed at the importance of reading to children, so maybe someone got that message. But I really learned the importance of planning, getting support, and the fact that no matter how great a program is, if no one knows about it, you will have a lot of empty seats!

In your publicity and marketing, use any or all of the following methods (see sample library flyers and training schedules in Appendix C):

- Training information on the library Web site
- Online calendar
- Library newsletter
- Newspaper
- Library blog
- Community weeklies
- Direct mailings
- Posters
- Displays
- Flyers in community gathering spots

- Press releases

- Public service announcements

- Signs on the library bookshelves

One great marketing idea was implemented at the Parker Public Library, a rural library in Parker, Arizona. The director, Jana Ponce, received a grant for a wireless laptop lab to provide computer training to the public. Her bright idea was to market in the local café. She asked the café owners if the library could provide the cafe's normal paper placemats. Using legal-sized paper, she printed the library event calendar and listed the workshop descriptions. This was a great low-cost method to get the word out to the entire community, including many people who did not regularly use the library. She said many people showed up at the library with their folded placemats, maybe a little sticky with syrup, but with the classes they wanted to take circled. What an unusual and smart way to publicize!

### Registrations

Many library technology trainers say that, once the word gets out, they have waiting lists of people wanting to take a computer class—so marketing isn't a problem. What might be a problem here is how to handle the overflow. Some libraries find it helpful to phone or e-mail participants the day before class, while others use an online registration program. One affordable example is from E•vanced Solutions (www.e-vancedsolutions.com), which offers online room reservations, event registrations, summer reading program management, and an online calendar of events with registration links. The program automatically moves people who are standbys to registered participants when space is available.

Whatever method you use, low- or high-tech, it is important to plan this process and evaluate how it is working. It doesn't need to be complicated, but you also don't want to spend too much valuable staff time or to have a workshop with too many empty seats.

---

### Survey Question: How Do You Publicize Your Workshops?

*Sarah Houghton-Jan, Information and Web Services Manager, San Mateo County Library, San Mateo (CA)* – "Workshops are publicized through our online calendar, flyers in and outside the library, and through outreach events. For an example of a typical flyer, see www.smcl.org/libraries/mil/events/images/COMPUTER-CLASS.jpg (we have a great graphic designer)."

*Bernadette Rivard, Supervisor of Technical Services, Milford Town Library, Milford (MA)* – "We publicize through our Web site (www.milfordtownlibrary.org/computerworkshops.html), which has a link to a sign-up survey sheet. We also have information about the classes in our weekly local newspaper column."

---

## Endnotes

1. Linda Honold, *Developing Employees Who Love to Learn: Tools, Strategies, and Programs for Promoting Learning at Work*, Palo Alto, CA: Davies-Black Pub, 2000: 31.

# Chapter 8

# Organizing and Designing the Workshop

*I never teach my pupils. I only attempt to provide the conditions in which they can learn.*
—Albert Einstein

As an accidental technology trainer, it can be frustrating to realize that, while you could spend a week delivering an introductory lesson, you only have 30 minutes of class time. How do you trim your topic down to the essentials? How do you get organized?

## Workshop Plan

A number of complicated texts cover designing curricula based on formal educational theories and requirements. While there is certainly merit in these studies, we should avoid making designing a workshop more complicated than it needs to be. This does, of course, require planning. You need to have an outline, creating a logical strategy to help you move smoothly through your workshop goals and organize your training ideas. You do not, however, need to be as formal as in a traditional lesson plan, and scripts can often be too limiting. You don't ever want to read pages of text to a class, unless you really want to give them time for a nice nap.

Your workshop plan should always be flexible. This is a guide to help you brainstorm how your workshop will emerge; it does not obligate you. Every workshop you facilitate should unfold differently, based on the people you are training. In your outline you merely select specific goals, determine the best techniques to use, and estimate timing to best help participants achieve the intended outcomes. Your plan will help you identify specific learning objectives, equipment requirements, and activities, preventing training from becoming haphazard and disorganized. You can determine how the workshop should flow, how the concepts logically fit together and combine to create the big picture (see Figure 8.1 for workshop plan components).

By using either a brief workshop plan or a comprehensive outline, trainers can organize their workshops and share their planning with other co-workers. Some libraries like to include sufficient details so that a different trainer could teach the workshop without having to start from scratch. I don't believe in standardized curricula; every trainer needs to make a topic and a workshop "their own" by incorporating their individual strengths, knowledge, and skills. However, sharing outlines and materials is a great way to learn.

Your planning should always focus on the participants. Remember you are training people, not delivering information. Your workshop content is worthless if no one can understand it,

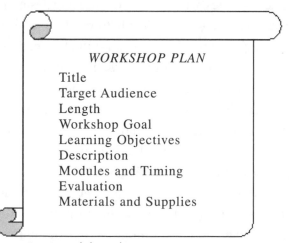

*WORKSHOP PLAN*

Title
Target Audience
Length
Workshop Goal
Learning Objectives
Description
Modules and Timing
Evaluation
Materials and Supplies

Figure 8.1   Workshop Plan

follow it, or remember it. You need a beginning, a middle, and an
end. (Actually, you need a lot of them, but we will get to that in a
minute.) A sample workshop plan template is included in
Appendix C, and some basics are outlined here:

- *Title* – Your titles can be catchy, but they must also be
  descriptive. You don't want a title that people don't
  understand.

- *Target audience* – How many people? Do you need to
  limit attendance? How many computers do you have?
  Could participants double up? Do you need to specify a
  skill level or prerequisites?

- *Length* – Can this workshop be done in an hour? Do you
  need less time or more?

- *Workshop goal* – What do you most want the workshop to
  achieve? Does it help support your library's strategic plan?

- *Learning objectives* – These may be stated as behavioral
  objectives (what the participant is expected to be able to
  *do* upon completion of the lesson) or as knowledge
  objectives (what the participant is expected to *know*
  upon completion of the lesson).

- *Description* – In a paragraph, describe this workshop. This
  can be used for marketing purposes. Will it be hands-on?
  Why would someone want to attend? Make it relevant.

- *Modules and timing* – Determine content. What will need
  to be learned to meet the objectives. Organize the content by outlining the sequence of events, with simple
  tasks first. This part also includes the training techniques
  that will be used.

- *Evaluation* – This may take the form of a set of questions
  to be answered. The evaluation measures whether the
  objectives were reached.

- *Materials and supplies* – Includes technology, handouts, PowerPoint, markers, coffee, and anything else you might need for the workshop.

Max Anderson, Educational Services Librarian, SOLINET, Atlanta (GA) shares his techniques:

> I start by writing out what I would like to cover, no matter the length of the class. (If I have too much content, this could mean a Part II!) Even if I don't plan on using PowerPoint for presentation purposes, I sometimes use it to start a sort of outline. For me, just writing out an outline in Word or even by hand doesn't work as well. I like the way I can add slides and move them around; it helps me get a better idea of what I should cover. Sometimes I have way too little content or way too much content. I try to do a dry run of a class well ahead of the published schedule. This way, if I find I have too little/much content or the exercises don't work, or there aren't enough exercises, I have time to modify it.

## Learning Objectives

The most important step in designing a workshop is establishing its learning objectives. This can be as easy as determining the top three things participants should learn during the training. Learning objectives are one of my favorite things! Once I really understood them, they have made workshop planning so much easier, and my training more effective.

I recently talked to a librarian friend at a small public library. The library had just implemented a new automation system and a trainer from the vendor came out to train staff how to use it. There were only a few computers and about six staff members. The trainer gathered them all around one computer while he demonstrated the applications. Some of the staff couldn't even see the screen. All of the training was conducted this way, with no hands-on activities. The next day, my friend went into work and found the staff in a tizzy. No one knew how to check out a book using the new system! The trainer had given them a lot of information, but never had them do it for themselves. As a result, the next day on the job they couldn't complete the simplest of tasks.

In an introductory level technology workshop, it is important to think in terms of the absolute essentials. When I was a trainer for the Bill & Melinda Gates Foundation traveling to small libraries around the country delivering introductory computer workshops, we never knew what skills we could expect from the library staff. In the first round of states, there were some rural libraries where no one in the session had ever touched a computer before. Although we had numerous lesson plans to cover regarding the software and maintenance, we would have to streamline our training to focus on the basics.

When we left, we knew that everyone had to be able to do three things: 1) turn on the computer, 2) log on to the computer, and 3) turn off the computer. This sounds simplistic, but sometimes it was evident that, if we could accomplish that much, at least the computers would be available to patrons. If we got staff through those three steps, then we could work on opening a program. But, while we would have them practice typing letters in Word and searching for articles in Microsoft Encarta, we knew that when we left everything else would be useless unless they could remember how to turn that computer on and off. It might not have been fun for either the trainers or the participants to go over the basic steps again and again, but it was necessary.

When determining learning objectives, really all you are doing is specifying what learners should be able to do as a result of participating in the workshop. What are the knowledge, skills, abilities, capacities, or attitudes participants should acquire or change in the workshop? You don't need more than a few objectives for each hour of a class. Think about what you *really* want them to accomplish.

For example, if you are teaching a one-hour "Introduction to the Internet" class, what do you want participants to walk away knowing how to do? Open a browser, type a URL in the address bar, and do a Google search? Leave out the history of the Internet dating back to ARPANET. There will always be more to teach than you have time to cover; learning objectives can help you narrow in on what is most important.

A good tool for forming objectives was developed in the 1950s by Benjamin Bloom. Years ago, when I was first introduced to Bloom's Taxonomy, it didn't really make sense to me. Now that I see how it works, I am finally relying on it, primarily to incorporate appropriate action verbs to ensure my objectives guide me in designing my classes toward the correct level of accomplishment.

Bloom's Taxonomy of Educational Objectives[1] is useful in classifying learning objectives according to the skill level required to meet them. Categories are formulated for three domains: cognitive (knowledge, thinking, and problem-solving skills), affective (attitudes, value systems), and psychomotor (manual or physical skills). Trainers often refer to these three domains as KSA (**K**nowledge, **S**kills, and **A**ttitude). This taxonomy of learning behaviors can be thought of as the goals of the training process: what new skills, knowledge, and/or attitudes the participants should acquire during the workshop.

Bloom's six levels are arranged in order of increasing complexity (1=low, 6=high). Levels 4–6 are known as the higher-level (or higher-order) thinking skills. The taxonomy of categories is:

1. *Knowledge* – Recalling or remembering information without necessarily understanding it. Includes behaviors such as repeating verbatim, describing, listing, stating, identifying, and labeling.

2. *Comprehension* – Understanding learned material. Includes behaviors such as demonstrating understanding of terms and concepts, explaining, discussing, and interpreting.

3. *Application* – Applying learned information to solve a problem. Includes behaviors such as demonstrating, solving, showing, and making use of information.

4. *Analysis* – Breaking down information into its elements to see interrelationships, ideas, and logic models. Related behaviors include differentiating, comparing, and categorizing.

5. *Synthesis* – The ability to put parts together to create something original. It involves using creativity to compose or design something new.

6. *Evaluation* – Judging the value of evidence based on definite criteria. Behaviors related to evaluation include determining, selecting, concluding, critiquing, prioritizing, and recommending.

I use behavioral verbs when writing my learning objectives. Use Table 8.1 to see which verbs are associated with each level of learning.

Learning objectives are also great to include in your marketing materials for workshops. This lets participants know what the expectations are, which will help them self-select appropriate classes. Always review objectives with participants at the beginning of every workshop, and get input to see if they are correct. Is there anything else important that should be included? Good learning objectives assist in planning, focusing the content, organizing the modules, and estimating the length of the workshop.

Here are some helpful questions to keep in mind when generating learning objectives:

- What are the demographics of your learners?

- What are their goals and motivation in taking this workshop?

- What are their expectations?

- What is their experience with technology?

- What is the skill or knowledge level of your learners?

- How will they use the information? Work? Home? Both?

- How can you address different learning styles?

Table 8.1   Bloom's Taxonomy: Behavioral Verbs

| Bloom's Taxonomy: Behavioral Verbs | | | | | |
|---|---|---|---|---|---|
| **Knowledge** | **Comprehension** | **Application** | **Analysis** | **Synthesis** | **Evaluation** |
| Arrange | Choose | Apply | Analyze | Arrange | Appraise |
| Define | Describe | Demonstrate | Calculate | Assemble | Assess |
| Identify | Determine | Dramatize | Categorize | Collect | Choose |
| List | Differentiate | Employ | Compare | Compose | Compare |
| Match | Discuss | Generalize | Conclude | Construct | Critique |
| Memorize | Explain | Illustrate | Contrast | Create | Estimate |
| Name | Identify | Interpret | Criticize | Design | Evaluate |
| Order | Interpret | Operate | Debate | Develop | Justify |
| Recall | Locate | Practice | Determine | Devise | Measure |
| Relate | Pick | Relate | Develop | Manage | Rate |
| Repeat | Practice | Schedule | Diagram | Modify | Revise |
| Select | Recognize | Shop | Distinguish | Organize | Score |
| Underline | Report | Solve | Estimate | Plan | Select |
| | Respond | Use | Evaluate | Predict | Test |
| | Restate | Utilize | Examine | Prepare | Validate |
| | Review | Initiate | Infer | Produce | Value |
| | Select | | Question | Reconstruct | |
| | Simulate | | Relate | Set-up | |
| | Tell | | Solve | Synthesize | |
| | | | Test | Systematize | |

Here are examples of learning objectives for three different workshops:

1. Learning Objectives for a 3-hour Beginning Level Workshop on Emerging Technologies for Library Staff:

   - *Explain* reasons libraries should care about social software
   - *Define* Web 2.0 terminology
   - *Explain* examples of emerging technologies
   - *Practice* using emerging technologies such as blogs, wikis, YouTube, and aggregators
   - *Indicate* increased confidence and comfort levels with using new technology tools

2. Learning Objectives for a 3-hour Beginning Level Workshop on Creating Your First Blog

   - *Define* blog and RSS
   - *Identify* reasons for having a blog
   - *Analyze* existing blogs and select favorites
   - *Create* a blog
   - *Apply* guidelines for effective blogging
   - *Develop* an action plan for continued use of blogs

3. Learning Objectives for a 1-hour Beginning Level Workshop on PowerPoint

   - *Identify* the PowerPoint program
   - *Describe* the basic features of the PowerPoint program
   - *Create* and select a presentation style
   - *Design* a short five-slide presentation

## Modules

By segmenting information into manageable sections, trainers can manage time well and increase their flexibility. This is sometimes referred to as chunking. Chunking is important for flexibility; technology training can resemble a reference interview, in that often the participants are not sure what they need when they sign up for a class or ask a seemingly simple question. They don't know what they don't know.

Psychological principles support the fact that learning occurs most effectively when instruction is doled out in small segments with time in between to process and practice; when links are made between new ideas and previous learning or experience; and when students are actively engaged with the material and with each other. To accomplish technology training that supports your objectives:

- Set small goals

- Develop small portions of content

- Use participant-centered activities

- Include as many hands-on and experiential opportunities as possible

- Be flexible and allow participants to achieve their own goals

Some of this has to do with the psychological principle known as primacy-recency, which is used by advertisers, writers, and entertainers. Many studies have focused on determining which items on a list are learned most easily and retained the longest. For example, if you give a person a list of words or numbers, the items most frequently memorized are the first item on the list (primacy) and the last item on the list (recency). What is learned first and last is best retained and recalled. In a 90-minute lecture without breaks, most of the material is presented somewhere in the vast cognitive wasteland of the middle. Make sure that the beginning and end of your workshops include important information (not just where the bathroom is and to turn off the computers on your way out), and build in additional beginnings and endings by incorporating shorter modules throughout your training.

A series of 15- to 20-minute modules, including participant-centered exercises for deeper processing of the new content, creates many more beginnings and endings. This results in more opportunities for better learning, especially better recall and retention. Participants learn more when you cover smaller amounts of material more thoroughly.

This seems apparent when you think of how we receive the majority of our information—short television and radio sound bites, blog posts, brief newspaper articles, concise Web sites, and quick podcasts. In a television sitcom or drama, you can barely watch for 10 minutes before there is a commercial break. A lengthy lecture will only give participants an opportunity to take a nap, think about what they need to do at home or work, or find some other distraction to their learning. Think about it like food; give them small, easy-to-digest bites. Training should be a series of appetizers, not a large, tough steak. Use our shorter attention spans to make training more effective.

Build each module around your learning objectives, incorporating appropriate learning materials, methods, and relevancy. Each module should be a separate component complete within itself that can be taught, measured, and evaluated or removed as a whole—one that is interchangeable with others and assembled into the whole picture. Focus on one concept at a time and include opportunities for participants to analyze and apply the concept.

### The First Module

The beginning of your workshop is your chance to get people's attention. This is your opportunity to make the case for why learners should *care* about the message you're about to communicate.

First-time novelists are often told to throw away their first chapter, because often the real action doesn't start until the second chapter. When I was in college, I remember my writing professor slashing out my first page with red ink every time I wrote an essay. What would happen if you removed the first 10 minutes of your presentation? Are you providing too much context? Things learners don't need to know? If you have an hour-long "Beginning Internet" class, don't delve into the history of the Internet and how routers and switches work. It is nice that you know, but it isn't going to help learners when they try to find a Web site for the first time on their own. Remember that the training is about them, not about you. Go ahead and acknowledge this; tell participants you are here for them, not to show off what you know, but because you want to help them learn.

Of course, you do have to begin with an introduction. Include any housekeeping information, such as where the bathrooms are, whether there will be a break (needed if your workshop is longer than an hour), food policies, and any ground rules. Make sure you emphasize that the workshop will be interactive and that mistakes are not failures, but ways we learn.

Your opening should catch participants' attention, and it should facilitate networking. Icebreakers are sometimes used for this purpose (find more on icebreakers in Chapter 5). A good icebreaker should allow people to introduce themselves *and* should relate to the topic. Make sure your icebreaker isn't a scary activity for shy participants, though; you want them to feel safe and secure.

If you have a manageable number of participants, give them the opportunity to introduce themselves and state why they signed up for the workshop. Introductions are important; one reason many adults attend training is for the social interaction. Intros will also help them participate in the workshop later, getting them past the hurdle of speaking for the first time in the group. Let them tell the group about their experiences, needs, and expectations.

Help participants focus on the skills or concepts to be covered. Place the technology in context; show them how it is being used. Show them an end product at the beginning of the workshop, so they can see what they are working toward. Meredith Farkas, Distance Learning Librarian, Norwich University, Northfield (VT), explains: "When covering any technology, I usually describe the technology, show how it is being used effectively in various settings and in various ways, and then I get into the nitty-gritty of how to get started using the technology and how to effectively implement it. I like to get them excited about the possibilities for using the technology before I get into the really practical stuff."

Your job is to interest participants in some way. Remember that people pay attention when they feel. Look at your first set of slides or your first few pages and ask yourself: "What feeling does this evoke?" Think of how novelists, screenwriters, great teachers, and even successful snake oil peddlers gain attention. Use one or more of the following to open with an impact:

- Begin with a question. Choose a question participants will want to have answered. In a good movie or novel, you find yourself curious about what will happen next. We can similarly make even dry technical topics fascinating. Find the passion. If you don't care about the subject, why should they?

- Lead with a story about real people or about a fictional character they can identify with.

- Start with something funny. Forget the advice to "open with a joke," unless you happen to be one of those rare funny people who can pull this off well. You don't have to start with a joke to get people laughing early. Sometimes a picture, story, or even just a quote can get them involved.

- How many bad books and movies have you finished just because you had to find out who did it? Look at your topic and find a way to set up a little mystery.

### The Middle Modules

Take each of your learning objectives and determine what training techniques would be most successful. Remember, variety is the spice of life! Include various activities throughout the workshop. Don't forget to build in time for breaks, which should be provided every hour. Let people stretch, get a drink, visit the bathroom. If they don't have personal comfort, the learning isn't going to happen. Can you provide coffee and water? Even better, can you give them chocolate?

Remember that, during activities, you still need to be engaged. It may be tempting to check your e-mail or zone out, but you need to be actively making sure everyone is doing well. I often notice that I don't get questions until I start walking around the room. Once I get near people, they feel more comfortable making eye contact and asking questions. I also ask them how they are doing or what they are discovering. Some people have no problem asking questions, but it does make others nervous, especially if it means attracting your attention (and that of the other participants).

### The Last Module

Just as you began on time, end on time—and try to end with a Big Finish. Remember, after a workshop, participants will remember best what they heard last. End by emphasizing important points, rather than just stopping abruptly. I've seen many trainers just trail off at the end, and the only way I knew the workshop was over was because they began packing up their bag.

It took me a while to really grasp the importance of a good closing. You want to make sure the participants realize that they learned—that they have been changed (or at least something in their brain has changed) by the experience. While this may sound simplistic, it is amazing how often they won't realize how far they have come unless you explicitly acknowledge it. In its simplest form, this is a summary, a clear picture of the overall learning that took place, but it works best if you can involve them. Ask people what they learned or use a review exercise. You want them to leave feeling confident and proud of what they've accomplished.

Don't just end with an evaluation sheet and a thank you for attending. Try to have some type of wrap-up. Review the learning objectives. Ask for questions. Review goals the learners had and ask if they were met. Ask the learners what they got out of the class. Have them share one thing they will use. Have them write down a few action steps for what they want to do when they leave, or how they will use what they've learned, or even what they want to learn next or how they will practice. Celebrate that they've done a great job. Thank them for their participation, time, and support of the library.

## Training Techniques

There are a lot of techniques you can use to vary your modules. Some of these include:

- *Lecture* – This is best used for delivering facts and background information.

- *Storytelling and examples* – Effectively weave narrative examples into your presentation. Illustrative stories can communicate pertinent messages with humor, insight, and the experience of the trainer. Reality-based examples allow the participants to see an immediate benefit.

- *Guided practice* – Participants follow along on their own computers while the trainer demonstrates. Participants progress as a group at a rate equal to that of the slowest student. It can be difficult to keep everyone together, but can be especially helpful with beginners.

- *Guided discussion method* – This is an interactive process of sharing information and experiences among the entire group of participants.

- *Group discussions* – Participants are divided into small groups (2–3 or 4–5 people, depending on the number of learners) to discuss topics or situations and then report back with a summary of their discussions to the entire class.

- *Q & A* – Questions and answers can be used several different ways. You can give the questions to participants and have them determine the answers, or you can let them come up with their own questions and answer them as a group.

- *Case studies* – You can give the participants an opportunity to think and discuss a real situation and how it may be relevant to them.

- *Learning games* – Games can be used to introduce, demonstrate, review, or apply concepts. The use of competition and a fun atmosphere can increase learner motivation.

- *Group projects* – Participants can work together toward a goal or to create a product. For example, they can create a blog, PowerPoint presentation, or flyer together.

- *Individual/self-paced exercises* – Participants work on their own to practice a skill or extend the knowledge on their own. You can create several versions that participants can choose from depending on their interests or knowledge level; maybe a print or Web-based exercise.

- *Independent practice* – This allows participants to explore and work on their own, and is usually very well received. The trainer can provide assistance and feedback.

- *Role-playing* – Role-plays or skits can be useful to demonstrate how something should or should not be done, the results, or adding context. *Never* assign a role to a participant who hasn't volunteered.

- *Demonstration* – The trainer shows the participants how a program can be used, examples of completed projects, or how to complete certain tasks.

- *Reflection* – A little quiet time gives participants an opportunity to contemplate what they've learned and how they may use it. This could be accomplished by having participants complete an action plan.

- *Panels or guest speakers* – Bringing experts into the workshop to show how they've used the technology or to teach a specific module can bring another perspective into the workshop and also demonstrate relevance. This can also be accomplished via a Webcast.

- *Videos* – Videos can be incorporated to provide visual interest or an interview by an expert. YouTube provides many free, entertaining videos that may be applicable.

- *DIY learning* – This is a Learning 2.0 type of exercise, based on self-discovery and personalized by the participant, with opportunities for social interaction and discussion.

- *Technology* – Incorporate other technology into the workshop. Create a Web site containing all the information and links participants need to follow in the workshop. You can have participants use blogs, wikis, online tutorials, or other Web sites for research and exploration.

Any time you can demonstrate, rather than just explain, do so. Any time you can have a hands-on activity rather than just a demonstration, do it. Do not, though, give instructions for an assignment and then keep talking while people are working; this is very distracting. Do not let discussions go too long. Make sure when giving time for reporting out or having a discussion that you let the group know how long you've allocated. If you want each group to report and you have five groups and 10 minutes, that is two minutes per group. Let them know that, or else you might get a talker who takes five minutes and throws off your schedule. You can even have a timer that goes off or use an online timer.

No class is ever the same. Each workshop will benefit from the individual experiences of each learner. This is part of what makes training a fun adventure.

## Evaluation

Your evaluation measures how successful you were in reaching your goals. You can see areas for improvement for yourself and find out whether the participants actually learned what you had intended. Your evaluation should be tied directly to your learning objectives, and you should also always provide an opportunity for participants to write their own comments and suggestions. It really doesn't need to be complicated! (See Chapter 7 for more on evaluation processes and models.)

Figure 8.2 shows a sample of a typical workshop evaluation form. We will use the example of the three-hour beginning level "Workshop on Emerging Technologies for Library Staff," with the learning objectives described on page 143.

---

**Evaluation Form**

*Emerging Technologies for Library Staff*

Date and Location

The objectives of this workshop were that participants will be able to:

>   *Explain* reasons libraries should care about social software
>
>   *Define* Web 2.0 terminology
>
>   *Explain* examples of emerging technologies
>
>   *Practice* using emerging technologies such as blogs, wikis, YouTube and aggregators.
>
>   *Indicate* increased confidence and comfort levels with using new technology tools.

On a scale of one to five, rate:

1. How well were the objectives achieved?

2. Overall quality of the program?

3. Presentations by trainer(s)?

Comments and suggestions:

1. Please answer at least one of the questions below. Describe a way(s) in which your knowledge or attitude or skills or behavior have been (or will be) changed by something you learned at this workshop.

   • Knowledge: I will use the following knowledge learned at this workshop:

   • Attitude: I have changed my way of thinking about:

   • Skills: I have the following new skill to use:

   • Behavior: I will implement the following new behavior:

2. We would like your suggestions in order to plan future workshops and training sessions. Please list your top training needs:

Thank you for your valuable feedback. It is helpful in planning and improving our training program.

---

Figure 8.2   Typical Workshop Evaluation Form

## Supporting Materials

Font size/handwriting must be large enough to be read in the back of the room; also, make sure you don't block the screen or flipchart and that you place it in easy view. Use colors, photos, and/or graphs. These should be concise, not crowded with information and graphics. Remember that any visual should help with learning and retention.

### Handouts

In technology training, handouts are very important. You don't need to spend hours designing step-by-step instructions. But you will need to provide basic information that participants can refer to later. Otherwise, some learners will fall behind as they struggle to write down all the instructions. Knowing they have a guide for future use makes people more comfortable, and visual learners can read handouts later and get information through charts, screen captures, and other visuals.

Organize the handouts ahead of time. There is no reason to waste time and distract participants by handing out five sheets at different times. Some trainers don't want to give out handouts at the beginning of the workshop because participants might read ahead—but if they learn that way, why not? Either way, make sure you are quick about distribution. Place handouts on the chairs or tables ahead of time, or ask someone to help pass them out.

One useful handout includes some type of agenda, without exact times. If you tell people that there will a break from 2 to 2:15, and are in the middle of an exercise at 2, some students may try to hold you to it—or just get nervous that you've forgotten and they won't get a break at all. Handouts can also be takeaways to help people learn and reinforce the information. Make a handout with Web sites, books, and articles they can access for free later; bring in relevant books they could check out. Create or print out quick guides they can refer to when they go home.

### PowerPoint Presentations

Think of the information on your slides as headlines, subheadings, or bullet points; use as few words as possible on each slide. A PowerPoint should reinforce what you say, not repeat it. Don't read your slides; this is *not* a teleprompter! Use interesting photos or clipart, and show how the technology you are covering can be used. Use slide transitions, blinking and moving images, and sounds only sparingly, as they can be very distracting. PowerPoints can aid visual learners, help you stay on task, and be a good communication tool if used properly.

### Flipcharts

Make flipchart headings in advance, so you won't waste time in class by turning your back to everyone while you write. Don't record participant output on a flipchart if it will not be used. Flipcharts can be great for teams to use when reporting to the group after an activity.

## Administrative Details

Successful workshops always involve a lot of small details. Managers and participants often don't realize how much time it takes to prepare for a workshop. See if you can have someone help you and divvy up some of these responsibilities; a volunteer or student aide could be very, very useful. It still amazes me how much time the administrative details of training require: registrations, copying handouts, moving tables and chairs, figuring out projectors. (I wonder how many times I have lost my Internet connection during a workshop!) See the sidebar on page 156 for some thoughts to help you plan.

Always start on time. Get to your workshop location an hour in advance. This might seem like overkill, but you never know what you might need to deal with before the workshop begins. I've had problems with traffic, been unable to get into a computer lab, found missing equipment, had equipment problems, no tables, no chairs, dirty tables—and even had the experience of no one at the library knowing about the event!

## Preparation Checklist

### Before

Develop a roster of learners and a sign-in sheet

Contact learners with confirmation and directions, time, and location

Pre-assessments

Make handouts and copies

Make evaluation forms

Make name tents (www.trainerswarehouse.com has some great dry erase ones)

Verify classroom location and setup

Get names and contact information for technical support

Order any audiovisual equipment you need, such as a projector or laptop

Design a PowerPoint, if necessary

Coordinate food and beverages

Gather supplies (markers, stapler, etc.)

Create certificates of completion

### After

Collect and compile evaluation forms

Clean up classroom and return any A/V supplies

Distribute evaluation summary to administration, committee, etc.

Address any questions not answered or any other follow-up

Next, do anything you can to create a comfortable and friendly learning environment. Make sure the room is as clean as you can make it (I keep a good supply of wet wipes with me, so I can quickly clean off tables). Arrange tables, if you can, and add color to the room with flipcharts, posters, tablecloths, markers, and toys. Yes, it *is* a trainer's job to clean and to haul. I was once asked when moving tables around if that was in my job description. My answer was yes—if you are a trainer, setting the environment is part of your responsibilities. Provide water and coffee if possible; of course, snacks and chocolate are even better.

As participants are arriving, make sure you try to greet them and make contact with them. Make them feel welcome. Try to address any comfort needs they have.

---

### Ten Tips for Preparation

1. Be early
2. Clean and set up the room
3. Look in the mirror
4. Test your technology, Internet connection, etc.
5. Greet people as they arrive
6. Set out your materials, sign-in sheet, name tents, pens, etc.
7. Have water and refreshments, trash cans, tissues
8. Know how to contact your resource people—especially tech support
9. Remember to focus on the participants
10. Think positively, and have fun!

---

## Common Training Tools

Beyond just computers, tables, and chairs, what tools are helpful for a trainer?

- Handouts
- Post-it notes

- Markers

- Name tents/name tags

- Flipcharts

- Flipchart stands

- Tape

- Stapler

- Drinks/food

- Music

- Projector

- Carts (I love the pack and roll carts, about $20 at office supply stores)

- Wireless projector remote control

- TV for videos or DVDs

- Puzzles

- Learning toys, such as pipe cleaners, stress balls, squeeze toys, anything to enliven learning, stimulate the senses and keep learners engaged (kinesthetic learners will focus better and absorb your material more quickly if they have something to do with their hands)

## Endnotes

1. Benjamin S. Bloom, *Taxonomy of Educational Objectives, Handbook I: The Cognitive Domain*, New York: David McKay Co. Inc., 1956: 3.

Chapter 9

# Dealing with Difficult Library Training Situations

*Why does Sea World have a seafood restaurant??*
*I'm halfway through my fish burger and I realize,*
*Oh my God ... I could be eating a slow learner.*
          —Lynda Montgomery

Accidental library trainers experience many difficult situations. These include the need to deal with varied skill levels, difficult trainees, technology failures, and registration problems. Let's look at how to stay cool under pressure, how to deal with specific problems that can arise, and how to create a toolkit of solutions to rely on. If you can't control the difficult situation, you will lose your authority and credibility, and the patience of your participants.

## Challenging Participants

As Malcolm Knowles wrote in 1950, "Not all adults are mature, and probably every adult is immature in some respects."[1] Try to remember that people aren't the problem, just their behavior. You can't change who they are, but you can encourage them to change their behavior. First try to identify what the issue is about. Is it a training issue, or is it a personal issue? Are they falling asleep because they are bored or they don't want to be there, or perhaps they just have a cold and are on medication?

You must deal with the behavior of a difficult participant. This lesson hit home for me while conducting a weeklong workshop.

The class contained a very monopolizing, negative person. As a trainer, I wasn't sure what to do about it and kept hoping they would just stop being such a problem. Someone else in the workshop finally approached me and asked me to do something about the domineering person, since it was affecting all of the participants. Don't let your problems get that far! If it is uncomfortable for you, it is uncomfortable for the whole room.

You need to make the training experience as safe and comfortable for everyone as possible. Sometimes, people seem challenging, but they might just need attention or to have a certain issue addressed. Often they just need their expertise acknowledged or their energy redirected.

"Difficult" doesn't just mean "annoying." To be successful in learning, someone may have to admit failure, display a lack of knowledge, or make mistakes. People who have been out of school for a long time or who didn't do well in school may be frightened at the thought of going to a workshop. But really, they have been learning all along. Advertise it as "trying something new."

### Setting Ground Rules

Communicating ground rules at the beginning of the workshop can be very helpful in creating a safe environment. You don't, though, want to start a workshop with a *lot* of rules. If you have the participants create ground rules, they will usually be tougher on themselves than you would. This can be an easy and fast exercise—just have participants call out any ground rules, and make a list. Make sure you get agreement from everyone before you adopt them for the workshop.

### Advanced Learners

Advanced learners are obviously knowledgeable and often disrupt the workshop by asking questions about topics that haven't been discussed yet. Try to involve them. Ask them to be a coach to a struggling participant, ask them for examples, or provide them with self-directed exercises. Acknowledge that they are advanced, but make it clear that you must cover the basics that were advertised for the workshop, so that the other participants can learn as much as they already know. Consider asking if they would rather wait for an advanced workshop to be offered, if they seem very frustrated.

### The Slow Learner

Even if you specify skills and prerequisites ahead of time, you will still get a slow learner or two in your workshops. Make sure you try to be patient and encouraging. Empathize with them, and tell them that you are still learning new technology skills, too.

It can be helpful to provide them with basic exercises to focus on. You might be able to pair them with a more advanced participant or have an assistant trainer help out. During breaks, try to get them caught up if they are behind. Remember never to take their mouse from them or press keys for them, no matter how tempting it might be. You can change their computer's settings to slow down mouse tracking if they have a problem following the cursor.

### The Latecomer

To avoid latecomers, get a reminder out the day before the workshop. E-mail is easy, or make a few quick phone calls; ask a volunteer to help with reminders. Don't wait too long for tardy participants. I've delayed a workshop only to find the late arrivals are actually no-shows. Life happens, and a participant might be sick or have car trouble, a work emergency, or a family situation. You need to be respectful of those who are there on time.

Latecomers are another reason to begin the class with participant introductions or an icebreaker that they could miss without getting behind on the content. I hate to start a class on time, only to have five people show up late who then don't know the workshop objectives, haven't been introduced, and don't know the agenda. It really isn't fair to the participants who arrived on time if you then repeat everything you've already covered.

### The Quiet One

If you have a participant with a very quiet voice who asks a question or makes an introduction you can't hear, there are several things you can do. It's tempting to move closer to this person so you can hear them, but this may only result in them lowering their voice even more. If you move farther away, they may instinctively raise their voice. You can put your hand up to your ear to indicate you can't hear. You can quickly interject and ask if people in the back could hear what they said; if not, ask them to repeat their comment louder. You don't want to embarrass a quiet speaker, but you don't want them to not be heard either.

Quiet might also mean overwhelmed, so really be careful about trying to draw them out in front of the group. During a break, you can always ask them privately how things are going or what they think of the class. You don't even need to acknowledge that they are being quiet; they might just be concentrating. It isn't necessary that *everyone* speak.

### The Scowler

I have had several people in workshops who seemed to glare at me the entire time. At first, I used to wonder why they hated me so much! But often, these are the same people who give the most glowing evaluations, or even come up to me after the workshop to let me know how much they enjoyed it. I don't know if they are just concentrating or have had Botox injections, but try not to read too much into some signals you might get. Sometimes, nonverbal communication can be misleading.

### The Talker

These people love side conversations. Ask them a direct question, or even just ask the person next to them. Don't take it personally.

Usually they don't even realize how distracting they are being. I have been guilty of this, since I love to talk about what I'm learning, but I appreciate it if someone lets me know that I'm being a problem.

If they keep talking, tell them you are glad they are excited about the content, but that they are distracting the rest of the class. Promise to give them some free time for exploration, if they will just hang in with you until then. Or ask them what they are so excited about—sometimes it really is relevant. You can also try making eye contact or even just moving closer to them while you are speaking.

### The Monopolizer

Monopolizers were initially the hardest trainees for me to deal with. Try to interject with a summary of their views (whether you agree or not), and then ask others to respond. Or, acknowledge the value of their comment, then ask them to talk more with you at a break or when there is more time. It is fine to go ahead and say that you need to move on to the next topic, but that you appreciate their participation: *You bring up a good point, and we could probably spend a whole hour discussing it, but since we have only 30 minutes left, let's move on the next section*, or *Let's hear from someone else this time.* You can try calling on other participants by name, such as *Jody, what do you think the next step would be?*

You can follow up by commenting to monopolizers at a break or at lunch that you appreciate their knowledge, but want to give less knowledgeable participants a chance, too. Talking to people with problematic behaviors does not have to become a confrontation, and often the personal interest you take in them is enough to dissuade them from giving you a hard time.

Give monopolizers something constructive to do. I had one trainee in a weeklong class that started out by just overpowering the group. He obviously wanted to teach the class, and just talked and talked. At the end of the first day, I told him that I could see he had a lot to offer, and asked if he would help me out the rest of the week by being my assistant. He was overjoyed to be recognized and happy to do things like recording on a flipchart when groups reported out, announcing when breaks were over, and even distributing handouts. He was completely quiet as well! I was surprised at the transformation, but he felt he had been acknowledged.

### The Know-It-All

Again, know-it-alls often just want recognition. Acknowledge their contribution or advice. *Yes, you are right, that is one way to do it*, or *Thanks for sharing that example—you have a lot of experience in that area.* If they contradict you, try responding neutrally, by saying, *That hasn't been my experience*, or *Perhaps you can show me that during break.* If they are really advanced, consider redirecting them to another workshop.

### The Interrupter

Briefly answer the interrupter's question and break eye contact. Try the following: *If you have specific questions about how you would use this at work or in your personal life, let's discuss them at a break*, or *Wow, you have a lot of questions! I wish I had time to answer all of them, but we only have 30 minutes left in the class. I'd be happy to meet with you after class if your questions aren't answered through this training.*

Use a "Parking Lot" to collect questions you might not have time to answer or that don't fit into the agenda. This can be as simple as writing these questions on a flipchart or a whiteboard. Then, when and if you have time, you can "unpark" the discussion.

If they are off on a real tangent, try to refocus them on the workshop's goals and objectives. Try saying, *There is obviously interest in this discussion, but I'm concerned about our time, so let's continue this discussion at break or after class.* You can politely interject: *I'm sorry to interrupt, but we only have so much time. This is an interesting conversation, but let's address it offline. We have a lot more to cover and we want to end on time.*

### The One that Doesn't Want to Be There

Over the years, I have had situations arise where people for whatever reason just do not want to be there. Perhaps they are being "forced" to attend the class against their will. Maybe, once they get there, it's somehow a different topic than the one they signed up for. These are both difficult situations. If I can sense that either is the case after the class has already started, then I might have everyone take a short break and talk to this person on the side to find out what I can do to make the class work for them. Do your best to meet expectations, but you cannot please 100 percent of people 100 percent of the time.

When I worked for the Gates Foundation, I traveled to a small rural library to do a workshop for about four libraries. One woman announced in front of the class: "The first thing you should know about me is that I don't want to be here. I came out of retirement to work in the library because I love books and now they are getting these computers and say I have to use them. I don't want to use them so I'm retiring again, but they said I had to come to this workshop anyway. But I don't want to be here." Whew! I told her that I appreciated her being there and that it was too bad she was going back into retirement, and asked what she would do with her extra time. She told me she enjoyed reading mysteries, quilting, and visiting her grandkids. I took those clues and worked examples of online resources for those hobbies into the workshop's content. During some self-directed exploration time, she was excited to find Web sites about quilting and even found that she could trade quilt squares with other people all over the world.

By the end of the class, she was won over. I heard her say under her breath, "I gotta find out how to get us some more of these computers, they are going to be popular." I couldn't resist, and stopped the class to ask her to repeat what she had mumbled. She was happy to do so, now that she was so excited and confident with her new computer. Of course, it isn't always that "easy." But, you can see the power of trying to keep a good attitude and of making the workshop relevant to each individual.

### The Long Breaker

Participants may take a longer break than you specify. Make sure you do give a specific time to return, instead of just telling them to take a 15-minute break; you can even write the time they are to return on the board. Some trainers like to announce an unusual time to return, such as 2:37. You can announce the end of a break with music or a bell. You can use online timer countdowns for breaks (such as the free one available at html_help4u.tripod. com/javatime.html) or offer small rewards, so that those who return on time are entered in a drawing.

### Group Dynamics

Sometimes it seems as if the entire class is disruptive. Try not to get flustered. Use humor; flip the lights on and off, saying "Testing, 1-2-3, testing ..." Divide them into small groups to work on activities, and don't be too strict. They don't all have to be on the same screen all the time. Let them explore on their own. You could also change up the activities or the groups. If someone is dominating the whole class, switch to small group or paired activities. If small groups are having problems, switch to whole group or individual activities. I was once in a workshop that was centered on small group work. Many of the groups had real personal conflicts, and no learning was going on. I wished the trainer had disbanded the small groups and let us learn as one group or individually.

One benefit of a second trainer is that everyone in your class is going to be different, with varying personalities, skill levels, and learning styles. It is helpful to have someone else there to balance your strengths. When I train, I have a lot of energy and enthusiasm. I prefer training with someone who is calm, relaxed, and who has a quieter personality.

## Other Issues

Although participants can often be problematic, technology training also involves responding to other difficult situations—such as the technology itself! Here are a few other issues and solutions.

### Questions You Can't Answer

Always acknowledge it if you don't know the answer. Bad information will undermine your credibility. Share what you can, and promise to look into it and get back to them later. You can also answer with: "That's a good question, can anyone in the group answer it?"

You may also know the answer, but it's just not relevant to the topic or the group. With those situations, try these responses: *That question is beyond the scope of this topic, can we discuss it later?* or *That question would take too long to answer now, but I'd be happy to talk to you later.*

### Time of Day

The time a workshop occurs can definitely have an effect. If it is early, you may have people who *need* their coffee or who are late because of traffic or dropping children off at school. Try to begin with an icebreaker, so if people are late, they won't have missed crucial material.

If the workshop is after lunch, you may have sleepy participants. Whatever the time, be aware of your participants and whether they seem engaged. Build segments into your workshop, and plan for stretches, breaks, and activities that require some movement.

## Technology Failures

Start by trying to find out everything you can about the room and equipment you will be using. Try to find out who your technical support will be and meet them ahead of time, or inquire how to contact them if you run into problems. If you give instructions to a third party, something might get lost in translation.

Always have backup plans. Prepare for a lost Internet connection with screenshots and archived Web sites. Print your PowerPoint as handouts, load it onto the instructor workstation, and bring a copy saved on a memory stick as well. When you are planning your workshop, consider some of the technology problems that could happen and brainstorm solutions. Thinking through scenarios before they occur can help you be levelheaded and calm if problems occur.

## Registration Problems

Some libraries have problems with participants registering and not showing up. (One trainer reported a workshop where 75 percent of the people failed to show up!) A few libraries have solved this problem with a small refundable deposit fee that is returned at the beginning of the class. If people do not attend, their deposit (around $5) is donated to the library's Friends group. As long as this policy is very clear up front, there are few problems. You can also call or e-mail participants the day before; again, this can be a responsibility for a library volunteer.

Online registrations can be a big time saver as well. Some libraries use an online registration program, such as those from E•vanced Solutions (www.e-vancedsolutions.com), discussed in Chapter 7.

Some libraries create waiting lists for popular classes; others avoid the hassle. Mindy Johnson, Head of Adult Services, Camden County Library, Voorhees (NJ) explains: "We don't do waiting lists. We tell people if they want to come on the day of the class and see if there are any open spots, they can take that risk. Most of the time, one or two people don't show up. Waiting lists became too cumbersome and caused problems. We could always offer more, but we'd need more staff willing to teach." An anonymous survey respondent shares: "We used to do a whole nightmare of waiting lists and call backs but have changed to first come, first served. Take a number, it saves your seat, and come back when it is time for class."

### No Time to Create Handouts and Lesson Plans

Library technology trainers often lack sufficient time for workshop preparation and planning. One great way to save time is by partnering with other libraries and sharing handouts and lesson plans. You can also involve library volunteers in creating handouts; many teens would love to have this opportunity to contribute.

Also, look online for library resources that share this information. InfoPeople, WebJunction, and quite a few libraries are listed in Chapter 11, under "Resources for Training Materials." Remember that, while these are great resources, they can become even better if you begin sharing your handouts and lesson plans as well.

### No Budget for Training

Many libraries have no training budget. This does not mean, though, that you can't provide any training. There are many free online workshops available, and there are many people who would love to be volunteer trainers. (See Chapter 7 for more information about using volunteers, and see Chapter 10 for examples of innovative volunteer programs being used in other libraries.)

You can also apply for grants. Library associations offer grants for staff professional development, and other sources offer grants specifically for public or staff training. You could also include a training component for either staff or the public as part of your other library grant projects. Visit my Library Grants

Blog (librarygrants.blogspot.com) for an updated listing of library grant opportunities, many of which could be used for training or equipment grants.

## Varying Skill Levels

Again, be flexible. Don't ignore the situation; ask participants to be flexible as well. Acknowledge the situation and try to create some opportunities for people to work independently on their own projects. You can also have them work in pairs, either keeping the skill levels together, or matching a beginner with someone more advanced. If you have the time, create two versions of exercises, beginning and advanced, or brainstorm ways to make an activity more challenging.

If you have two trainers, consider dividing the class into two groups. I once had a workshop with some participants who had never touched a computer and others who were using Excel and other advanced software programs. Thankfully, I was with another trainer and we were able to form two smaller classes. One of us covered mouse basics, while the other went on to more advanced topics.

## Not Enough Time in Workshop

Never end a workshop later than the time that was planned and advertised. This is rude. Participants will leave feeling frustrated, rushed, and distracted about being late for a meeting or picking up their kids. You want them to leave the training with a positive feeling of accomplishment. End with: "This is what you accomplished/learned."

Planning your timing carefully is useful, but you can never be completely sure how long a segment will take. Interactions among participants and discussions are important, and should not be rushed. Keep your eye on the clock so you know when to move on to the next topic. I use a small digital clock that I take with me and prop up so I can easily glance at it.

If someone gets stumped, offer to spend more time with them later. You have to keep on schedule as much as possible. I recently taught two Emerging Technology workshops for staff at a local library. In the first workshop, there were lots of questions and interactions. This resulted in less time for individual explorations; instead, we learned as a group. In the second one, there were not as many questions, and many of the participants seemed to be at a beginner level. This created more time—30 minutes more!—for them to work on their own exploring social technologies. Both groups gave great evaluations, and both learned a lot, just through different methods. Sometimes you just have to be flexible and respond to what is working best for the participants in that particular workshop.

Never rush through a workshop just to cover all the content. It is better to leave out some tasks than to talk so fast that the participants are unable to keep up or learn anything from you. More words do not mean more learning.

### Bad Space

Some computer labs and training spaces are just not conducive to learning. You might experience bad lighting, noise, boring decor, pillars in the way, and not enough room. It might be hot, or cold, or both. You can try to add color through tablecloths and posters. Try to make sure the room is as clean and organized as it can be. You can use a theme and decorate to help add some creativity to an institutional-looking environment. Even bringing in some props from home or from the children's area of the library can make it look friendlier. Do your best to create an open, low-stress environment with the least number of distractions.

### Equipment Problems

Sometimes, no matter how much you plan, you can't know what is going to go wrong with your training room or equipment. The best you can do is the best you can do. Try to explain any equipment situations to the participants. Acknowledge the problem, and thank the participants at the beginning for being flexible. This puts the idea of being flexible into their minds. It is true that basic needs have to be met for training to really be effective, so if the room is really an uncomfortable temperature or overcrowded, or there is construction noise, your training will be affected.

When asked about the biggest obstacles for libraries offering technology training, Sarah Houghton-Jan, Information and Web Services Manager, San Mateo County Library (CA), responded: "Time and facilities are, by far, the biggest obstacles for libraries trying to offer technology training to the public. Most libraries still don't have separate walled-in computer labs where scheduling training is easy. As a result, classes take place before or after regular library hours, placing an undue burden on staff schedules. Time is also a factor. In the years of reduced staffing, reference staff are now being asked to do all their previous duties, plus training, plus dozens of other things. Preparing a training session and teaching it takes so much time—I don't think management has a good grasp of that fact."

All new trainers fear unexpected situations arising in their classrooms. Things do often go wrong in training, especially when technology is involved. But, with preparation and flexibility, you can always deal with it. Keep your cool and don't dwell on the situation; deal with it, and then move on to the learning.

---

### Survey Question: Give an Example of a Particularly Difficult Training Experience and How You Resolved the Issue

*Meredith Farkas, Distance Learning Librarian, Norwich University, Northfield (VT) – "I usually leave a lot of time for questions, because in my experience, when I give a talk I* usually have more questions than I have time to answer. One time I was giving a three-hour workshop on wikis, and I left about 25 minutes at the end for questions and discussion of specific applications people were thinking of. I think I ended up with five, maybe ten, minutes of questions, and then had at least fifteen minutes to fill. I actually ended up listing questions I commonly get at other talks that these people didn't ask and answered each of them. Certain populations just don't ask as many questions, so it's a good idea to have a list of questions you've been asked in the past to fill time, or at least have a plan for other topics to discuss if you have that time."

*Sarah Houghton-Jan, Information and Web Services Manager, San Mateo County Library, San Mateo (CA)* – "Every time you have a student who doesn't want to be there you have a difficult situation. The best way to handle these folks is to treat them with respect, even when they are being discourteous. Ask them meaningful questions, trying to engage them in the class. Approach them during a break to figure out what their problem with the class is. If they are only there because their supervisor made them, and are being disruptive and obstreperous as a result, send them home."

*Brenda Hough, Technology Coordinator, Northeast Kansas Library System, Lawrence (KS)* – "One of the biggest challenges in technology training is always the variety of skill and experience levels within a group. Some training participants may have no knowledge or experience with the topic and others may be fairly familiar with it. Addressing those disparities is a challenge. I try to resolve it by creating as many self-paced exercises as possible. I try to provide the context and some examples and then let the individuals work at their own pace. I can then be a guide on the side, helping each individual build independence and meet his or her needs."

*Max Anderson, Educational Services Librarian, SOLINET, Atlanta (GA)* – "I use a 'Parking Lot.' I will post a blank sheet of large paper in an area of the room. As we are going along in class, if someone asks something that is not usually covered in the class, I will 'park' it here. By the end of the day, my goal is to address what is parked there."

*Anonymous* – "I had to teach a class on a subject (eBay Selling) with which I was not comfortable, so we all walked through the sign-up process together. Luckily, I had some students in the class who had some limited experience, so we used their experience in a group discussion, as well."

## Endnotes

1. Malcolm Shepherd Knowles, *Informal Adult Education: A Guide for Administrators, Leaders, and Teachers*, New York: Association Press, 1950: 3.

## Chapter 10

# Examining Best Practices in Library Technology Training

*The mediocre teacher tells. The good teacher explains. The superior teacher demonstrates. The great teacher inspires.*
—William Arthur Ward

In the following sections, find advice and descriptions from library technology trainers around the country who showcase their best practices and their most popular workshops. Make your workshops more interesting by using library resources and community partners in your programming. Ideas from the "Hot Library Workshops" described here can be incorporated to keep your programming current, approachable, and relevant.

## Hot Library Workshops

Which are the hottest library workshops? The real answer is: It depends! It depends on the community—the skill levels and interests of participants—and on the library—what workshops are currently offered, what was done in the past, and the marketing methods used. This really comes back to the needs assessment outlined in Chapter 7; what your community wants will determine what is hot. Of course, with technology training, sometimes they don't know what they don't know, so make sure to offer a few experimental workshops once in a while and see if they are popular.

The following are some example workshops you might want to emulate.

### I Just Need 3 Sources by Tomorrow (www.library.ohiou.edu/workshops/3sources.html)

From Ohio University Libraries, this is an open-ended hour for students to bring whatever they are working on to a librarian and ask specific questions. Students will come away with exactly the source or two they need right now: expert, efficient, to-the-point instruction and activities. Preregistration is *not* required. Just come at the day and time listed.

### Fantastic Freebies for Everyone (www.princeton library.org/research/techcenter/classes.html)

From Janie Hermann, Princeton (NJ) Public Library. "Contrary to popular belief, there is such a thing as a 'free lunch' and you can find it on the Web. The number of free services, sites, and downloads is multiplying monthly at an astonishing rate in a new era of Internet innovation. This class will take you on a tour of some of the hottest freebies currently available. Everything from system tools to image editors to word processors and much more can all be found online for no cost. This session will ensure you know where to find the newest and most useful tools to keep you on the cutting edge of technology."

### Learning 2.0 Program, PLCMC, North Carolina (plcmc learning.blogspot.com)

The Public Library of Charlotte & Mecklenburg County (PLCMC) has amazing staff *and* public training. Note the variety of workshop topics and audiences for its public training.

Learning 2.0 was originally developed and launched by Public Services Technology Director Helene Blowers for the staff at the Public Library of Charlotte & Mecklenburg County in August 2006. A total of 352 people participated, and many additional guests joined in. Learning 2.0 is an online self-discovery program that encourages library employees to try new technologies, specifically Web 2.0 tools (blogs, wikis, podcasts, online applications, etc.), and rewards them for completing 23 "things" (or small exercises) on their own. Rewards included 117 MP3 players and a laptop. The program is built on the idea that participants learn best when they're engaged in their own learning and are motivated to learn. Read more about the program in the February 2007 issue of *Computers in Libraries* magazine (www.infotoday.com/cilmag/feb07/Blowers_Reed.shtml).

### Public Classes at ImaginOn (www.imaginon.org)

ImaginOn is a collaborative venture of the Public Library of Charlotte & Mecklenburg County and the Children's Theatre of Charlotte. Public classes include:

- *YouTube Video Contest* – Film and edit on-site with free help from staff and interns. Drop-in hours for ImaginOn's Studio-i: M–Th: 4–8:30 PM, Fri: Closed, Sat: 10 AM–5:30 PM (family time all day), Sun: 2–5:30 PM.

- *Take Photos for Your Webpage* – Got a MySpace, Facebook, or other online account? Need cool pics for it? The Loft can help! Just drop by The Loft on Thursdays 5–7 PM and they'll snap your picture for you.

- *Present Your Research* – Home school students sharpen research and presentation skills on a fascinating, self-selected topic at ImaginOn. This is a multipart class; please plan to attend all classes.

- *Teen Second Life: Get One!* – Explore the virtual world of Second Life. Learn from other teens how to build in 3-D, script objects, and interact with other avatars. Your world. Your imagination.

- *Make Your Own Computer Games* – Use Game Maker to create many different types of games. For ages 9–11. Participants should be familiar with using a mouse, dragging and dropping objects, and online game play. Creating games builds visual literacy, strategy, and symbolic recognition skills.

- *Gaming for Parents* – Learn why video and computer games are so popular and how they can benefit tweens and teens. This workshop will look at research, suggested games that are brain-power builders, and then you will also play a few games.

- *Scanning at the Library* – Virtual Village has equipment for scanning either text documents or images. Learn how to use this equipment at this workshop, plus get tips on how to improve the quality of scanned images. Be sure to bring pictures or documents that you'd like to scan. This class is designed for adults who have mastered basic computer skills.

- *E-mail by Appointment* – Having problems with creating that e-mail account? Come learn from staff with one-on-one appointments. Sessions will be 30 minutes long.

- *Computer Q&A* – Have questions about your computer that aren't covered by any of our regular workshops? Computer Q&A is an open forum-type group where your host will help you find the answers to your questions. Drop-ins welcome.

## Promoting Electronic Databases to City Staff Members

In January/February 2007, the *Marketing Library Services* newsletter published a cover story called "Promoting Electronic Databases to City Staff Members" (www.infotoday.com/mls/jan07/index.shtml). Chicago Public Library created a simple database-orientation program, which staff presented numerous times to city employees.

This was great PR for the library, plus attendees became advocates for the library. The city staff worked more efficiently with the databases and saved money by dropping some of their own expensive resources.

### Schenectady County Public Library Workshops

The library provides workshops that highlight its databases, often with topic-specific sessions. For example, the staff promotes NoveList to members of the community who belong to book clubs. They have investment resources workshops that feature databases that people may have heard about, but aren't quite sure how to use. They provide bookmarks with instructions on how to access the databases from homes or offices to promote remote usage.

### Today's Teens, Tomorrow's Techies

Brooklyn Public Library runs a program called "Today's Teens, Tomorrow's Techies." In this volunteer program, teens begin learning computer skills in a two-week technology institute over the summer. Then, they share those skills by helping patrons use library computers. Volunteers also assist library staff as lab assistants with computer troubleshooting and computer training workshops for the public. Teens volunteer a minimum of three hours per week for a period of at least six months.

### Geek Out, Don't Freak Out!

In an expert technology trainer interview for this book, Andrea Mercado, Reference & Techie Librarian, Reading (MA) Public Library, provides the following tips and instructions on an innovative workshop series:

> Before I was a librarian, I worked in technology, doing everything from technical writing to Web development to project management to technical support. When I first started working at Reading Public Library, my main

responsibilities included shifts on the Information Desk and teaching the computer classes, and my past life prepared me well for the position.

Since I'd never created my own class schedule or lesson plans before, I worked with what was already being done. The original schedule included such classics as basic Microsoft Office classes, using the library catalog, and researching medical issues. However, through my interactions with patrons in the classes and at the Information Desk, I found that our regular classes targeted a small and specific segment of our constituency, and that patrons regularly had questions about buying and using their various technology gadgets. It seemed a very logical step to offer classes about the items they asked about most, get them to *geek out* in a hands-on environment instead of *freaking out* about not knowing what to do. Besides, it also made the library and the librarians look super smart to know something about current technology *and* fill an information need.

Thus, the *Geek Out, Don't Freak Out!* series of classes was born: hands-on classes where patrons bring a gadget with the manual and a sense of adventure. I started with the most asked after gadget, digital cameras, created a handout chock-full of book titles on cameras and digital photography (mostly from our collection, including call numbers), articles (available in print or through our online resources), Web sites, and a glossary of useful terms.

I bring the books, copies of useful articles, and the library's digital cameras to the meeting, start the class with the caveat that I am not an expert, and that the purpose of the class is for us all to learn and figure it out *together*. We do quick introductions, and each person tells the group what they most would like to learn from the session. Most classes have at least one or two people who don't own a camera (or the featured gadget), and just want to know how to buy said gadget, so having an extra gadget on hand is really handy.

Then, things get delightfully crazy. We go over basics like parts of the camera, what all the little icons mean, taking a steady picture, flash settings, rechargeable battery issues, etc. It's a wonderfully social class, where people will just instinctively begin to help each other and chat amongst themselves, which I encourage. I also encourage people to bring friends who are good with cameras, so that we can learn from them, too. My class assistant(s) also help with the running around the room, showing things to people, and answering questions. When in doubt, I encourage people to check the manual or try one of the books on the table, which gets them in the habit of helping themselves later.

This class has been incredibly successful and is always in demand. If patrons had it their way, we'd offer it every month! We've expanded the series to include MP3 and digital audio players, since we now lend MP3 players for use with our Listen Up! Reading NetLibrary eAudiobook service. So far, the digital cameras class is still the big favorite. I'm hoping to expand the class to smartphones, personal digital assistants (PDAs), and any other gadget patrons start to ask us about.

### Technology Expo (thelibrary.springfield.missouri.org)

The Springfield-Greene County (MO) Library District has twice hosted a technology event sponsored by a local computer club, the Interactive Computer Owners' Network (ICON). This included seminars, exhibits, the latest digital toys, and a game room where visitors could play games on Microsoft's XBox 360 or the Nintendo Wii. A Google representative displayed Google Earth, a software program that uses satellite imagery to let users visually explore the world from their desktop. The library provided laptops to demonstrate programs such as OpenOffice (openoffice.org), a suite of programs similar to Microsoft Office that is available free online. Representatives from computer clubs for PC, Mac, and Linux users were there, but the most popular service was a computer health clinic. People were able to bring in their home computers, which volunteers would check for problems for free.

## Possible Technology Workshops for Staff and Patrons

The variety of workshops being offered by libraries is amazing. For some workshops, it is helpful to establish whether any prerequisites, such as mouse use or other basic skills, may be necessary. Be sure, though, that you don't require a prerequisite if it isn't really needed. For example, one library requires that everyone take a workshop on how to use the library's catalog *before* they can take any other library workshop. Now, this might make sense in some cases, but do people need those skills before they take a class on eBay? Before a Word class, if they just need to learn to write a letter or a resume? Even if this is a resource we (as librarians) may feel is very important, this is not a good enough reason for adult learners. Having to jump through the hoop of completing a prerequisite on a resource I don't have a need for, or already know how to use, would certainly deter me from taking a workshop I'd otherwise be interested in.

Here is an extensive list of workshop titles that libraries are offering, which may help provide you with inspiration and ideas:

*Technology Specific*

How to Purchase and Care for Your Computer

Using Digital Cameras

Sharing Photos Online

Photo Editing Boot Camp

Microsoft Office Programs: Word, Publisher, Excel, Access

Troubleshooting—Beginning and Advanced

Upgrading the Home Computer

Computer System Basics

Your Computer: What's Under the Hood?

Keyboard Shortcuts

Printing

Mac vs. Windows

Organizing Your Computer with Files and Folders

Setting Up a Wireless Network At Home

*Subject Specific*

Reading Group Resources

Gardening Resources Online

Listening to Music Online

Travel Planning Online

Genealogy Online

Online Sales and Shopping With eBay

Savvy Online Shopping

Wedding Planning Online

Genealogy Online

Quilting Resources Online

Anime

Online Recipes

Pregnancy Resources

Homework Help

Online Book Sales

Making Holiday Cards

Making Holiday Newsletters
Applying for Colleges
Consumer Technologies
Online Local History Resources

*Social Software Topics*
Blogs and Blogging
Dating Online
MySpace
IM (instant messaging) and Chat
Wikis
Second Life
Gaming
YouTube
Tagging
Del.icio.us
Flickr
LibraryThing
Skype

*Internet Safety*
Spyware, Plugins, and Popups
Internet Safety for Parents and Kids
Cookies and Viruses

*Business/Job Related*
PowerPoint for Professional Presentations
Tax and Accounting Software Programs (such as Quicken or
    TurboTax)
Job Hunting
Creating Resumes
Completing Online Applications
Investing Online
E-mail

    Economic Forecasts

    Desktop Publishing—for Business, for Teachers, for Fun

    Grant Workshops

*Home Related*

    Buying Your First Home

    Protecting Your Credit

    Home Improvement Help Online

*Internet or Database Specific*

    How Do I Get Online?

    Web Searching

    Web Design

    Databases vs. Search Engines

    Online Research Techniques

    Library Catalog and Database Training

    Internet Search Secrets

    Google and Advanced Google

## Innovative Volunteer Programs

Some libraries find great success using volunteers to help with their technology training. These volunteers are often senior citizens, teens, or college students. Chicago Public Library, for example, started using college students as computer-training volunteers, and then developed a teen volunteer program called Cyber Navigators (www.chipublib.org/008subject/003cya/teened/tech37intro.html). High school juniors and seniors are trained by the library on technology and public service skills. The Cyber Navigators troubleshoot equipment, teach library users how to use electronic resources, and prepare selected Web site lists (called Webliographies). The program is funded by a grant from AT&T through the Chicago Public Library Foundation.

## The Netguides Program

Netguides is a teen volunteer program developed by Andrea Mercado at Reading Public Library in Massachusetts as a way to provide one-on-one technology help for the public. You can read more about Mercado's adventures with the Netguides on her blog, under the Netguides category (www.librarytechtonics.info/archives/netguides).

### How did you come up with this idea?

The idea stemmed from two places: the original incarnation of the program from many years ago, when students helped students understand the very nascent Internet and acquired community service hours; and the desire to provide patrons with more technology help than was usually physically feasible for librarians to offer at our very busy Information Desk.

### How does it work?

High school students are recruited through an application process (hopefully with time the program will expand to include retirees and other ages of volunteers). Accepted Netguides sign a contract committing to three one-hour training sessions (subjects include customer service skills, library class handouts, online resources, and finding information on the library Web site), as well as two hours of service per month over the course of four months.

Once trained, these students are then able to help staff and patrons in various types of interactions, on a rotating schedule:

- On-Call – A single Netguide is stationed near the Information Desk, where a librarian can find them when assistance is necessary (2 hour shift, 5 days/week).

- Drop-In – Several Netguides are available during scheduled sessions for the specific purpose of helping patrons who drop by the Computer Lab with questions (2–4 hours, once a month or as demand requires).

- Class Assistant – Several Netguides provide assistance to patrons in computer classes (1.5 hours twice a month).

- By Appointment – A single Netguide meets with a patron during a scheduled appointment to address a specific knowledge need (45 minutes).

## How do you keep it all straight?

The group is managed online via a private Yahoo! Group, where features like the Calendar, Messages, Files, Links, Polls, and Databases allow for easy, documented, online management of the group in an environment the volunteers very easily understand. The online group also allows for easy management by the part-time supervisor, as well as the ability for other staff members to access the group without permission from a gatekeeper.

## Do you have any tips for librarians who want to start their own Netguides Program?

- Assess what types of interactions you wish to offer to your patrons. It may be that you have staff and resources to offer appointments only, or on-call during certain days of the week.

- Be sure you have a plan for and a person available to manage, schedule, and promote for the long haul.

- Think out the program cycle before you start. What is the minimum hour and time frame commitment for volunteers? Do you want to train new volunteers every month or every four months? Can you swing your desired plan?

- When looking for volunteers, look within the groups in your community that a) have the time, and b) have the skills. You may find that there are way more active older adults in your community with tech skills who have the time to give rather than teens in search of National Honor Society community service and leadership opportunities.

- Select volunteers with a customer service mentality and a good learning curve. Teaching technology skills to an open brain is easier than changing an attitude or mindset.

- Evaluate! Be sure that patrons fill out an evaluation for the appointments and drop-in style interactions. Also, have your *volunteers* fill out evaluations of interactions, to get a sense of how they feel the work is going.

- Use your evaluations to arrange any necessary continuing education for your volunteers outside of the initial training, and to make changes to the program schedule/offerings/management as necessary.

## Tips from the Experts

**Survey question: Which classes are the most popular/HOT?**

*Max Anderson, Educational Services Librarian, SOLINET, Atlanta (GA)* – "SOLINET did a survey of the membership a couple of years ago to get a feel for how the members felt about our training offerings and what they wanted for the future. Topics that were considered 'hot' centered around any emerging technologies. This has proven true for scheduling as well. The most popular classes tend to be: technology, RFID, emerging trends in technology, and social software/Web 2.0. OCLC topics are also always popular, probably because people need them to do their jobs!"

*Bernadette Rivard, Supervisor of Technical Services, Milford Town Library, Milford (MA)* – "Every summer, we offer a different 'Computer Camp' workshop topic for kids of varying ages. Topics have included making a PowerPoint presentation about an animal and creating a wiki about places the kids have traveled."

*Helene Blowers, Technology Director, Public Library of Charlotte & Mecklenburg County, Charlotte (NC)* – "There's still a lot of need for basic PC skills classes for the public, but we're starting to see a lot of interest in new topics ... online photo editing, eBay, MySpace for Parents, etc. These classes help fill a need to acquire new knowledge for those who already have basic skills."

**Survey question: What is your advice to accidental library technology trainers?**
*Michael Porter, Community Associate, WebJunction, Seattle (WA)* – "Be brave, have fun, be yourself, know your subject matter, relate to the audience as a colleague/team member/friend/fellow human being."

*Anonymous* – "People like to see practical applications, they like to actually get their hands on the technology, and they want to know how to implement and use the technology. They get really frustrated with just a basic introduction to a technology tool without much of a practical focus on how to use it, or a focus on just one application of the tool that may not be applicable at their library. If at all possible, do your training sessions in a lab setting, because it's much easier to get people to understand what you're describing if they can actually use it. When you can't be in a lab setting, the best thing you can do is to actually show them the mechanics of the tool rather than just describing it. A live demo is worth a thousand words."

*Max Anderson, Educational Services Librarian, SOLINET, Atlanta (GA)* – "Practice your content in front of people not associated with the library (a friend, partner, spouse) so that you get a realistic idea of how to present it. Also, this will help you to determine if your exercises work or not!"

*Anonymous* – "Less is more. Keep[ing] it simple is better than overwhelming them. Pre-assessments (like a online survey through zoomerang.com) can help determine beforehand what the levels will be. Hands-on time is really good for adult learners."

*Sarah Houghton-Jan, Information and Web Services Manager, San Mateo County Library, San Mateo (CA)* – "Teach technology like you're teaching it to your mom. Be as patient as you would be with your mom, and even with the most complicated topics, try to find a way to explain it so that your mom would understand. (Note: This does not work if your mom is a techie herself.)"

*Anonymous* – "Keep your presentations short so that the majority of your time is in the application. Also, if the users have time limits on their cards, and you have the ability to give them more time, do that as soon as they sign into the application so you don't have to interrupt the class once you start."

*Brenda Hough, Technology Coordinator, Northeast Kansas Library System, Lawrence (KS)* – "Step back from the technology. Provide the context and the big picture first. What is the technology? How is it used? Then dive into the steps involved in using it."

*Anonymous* – "Try to remember what it was like the first time you used a computer. Let folks know that they can't really break the computer. There's nothing they can do that can't be undone."

*Chris Peters, Information Technology Specialist, Washington State Library, Olympia (WA)* – "Find someone to help you with logistics, setup, teardown, snacks, etc. Use small group exercises and hands-on exercises as much as possible."

*Anonymous* – "Clearly state what you will cover in the class before you start, and let students know how you will handle questions. This sets expectations for the class and can eliminate problems."

*Mindy Johnson, Head of Adult Services, Camden County Library, Voorhees (NJ)* – "You must have patience, patience, patience. Use a bit of humor, but don't overdo it. Emphasize that you were once a learner yourself and that you still learn new things every day."

*Anonymous* – "Make it fun! We had a blast preparing the presentations and went very wacky on some occasions. As a result, we were viewed as being approachable and 'not scary.'"

*Anonymous* – "You have to like the patrons and remember they know stuff you don't—even if it is not technology."

*Colleen Eggett, Training Coordinator, Utah State Library, Salt Lake City (UT)* – "Your enthusiasm must shine through. If you don't believe it, no one else will."

*Scott Hines, Reference Librarian, Pacific Graduate School of Psychology, Palo Alto (CA)* – "Never be afraid to say: 'I don't know, but I'll look it up and get back to you [in a minute, after the break, tomorrow, once I figure it out].' Your honesty and integrity will be communicated clearly so that everyone knows they can trust you for accuracy and you will avoid spreading inaccurate information by answering prematurely."

*Anonymous* – "It is so important to keep abreast of new technological developments. Read with voracity, make time to play and practice, and don't ever stop to take a break from it. Keep an eye out for trends, and be able to know when to let go. Technology is a moving target, and by the time you've mastered it, something better has come along. If you can accept this, you can succeed in moving with the trends."

*Erin James, Library Associate, Gwinnett County Public Library, Lilburn (GA)* – "(1) Patience. Most of the people I help are my parents' ages (I'm 26, they're 50+). (2) My personal favorite idea is to teach people to 'Try it.' When they hesitate on where to click, or why, or what if they do this or that—I say calmly, 'Just try it.' Sometimes I know what will happen, sometimes I don't. Either way, it gives me the opportunity to help them learn to navigate. If it was the right place to click, they're ready for the next step. If it wasn't: 'This doesn't look right, does it? How do we get back to where we were? What might be a better choice?' They start to pick up that alarms won't go off and the computer won't melt down."

*Mary Bucher Ross, training consultant, Seattle (WA)* – "Make sure that your focus is on what is learned, not on what you taught. I have seen too many trainers plan to cover too much content in the time allocated. When they run short on time, they speed up their delivery, in order to cover everything they planned. The learners are better served by attention to and pacing for their needs, and by more opportunities for practicing the new skills. At the end of the class what is more important: what you taught, or what they learned?"

## Chapter 11

# Keeping Current and Sharing Resources

> *Live as if you were to die tomorrow. Learn as if you were to live forever.*
>
> —Mahatma Gandhi

With any topic, it is important to stay current and keep your workshops from becoming stagnant. Keep them fresh by finding help and inspiration in sources such as blogs, e-mail discussion lists, Web sites, and print resources. Many libraries are also sharing handouts, PowerPoint presentations, and workshop outlines.

## Ways to Keep Current

You have many options for staying current on new technologies and learning training tips, and for helping others in your library do so as well. Create your own learning toolbox, including books, journals, technology, classes, mentors, and Web sites. Here are a few ideas:

- *Lunch and learn* – Gather staff during lunch time for technology discussion or show and tell.

- *Coaching or learning partners* – Team staff members together for learning.

- *Conferences* – Both attending and presenting at conferences will keep you up-to-date.

- *Demonstrations* – Demonstrate ways to use technology in your staff room or lab.

- *15 minutes of learning* – Assign yourself 15 minutes a day or per week for learning.

- *Professional meetings* – Find out about library groups in your state and join.

- *Mentoring* – Find a mentor or be a mentor.

- *Projects* – Work with other staff or volunteers on technology projects.

- *Research and writing* – You can learn a lot by doing research or writing an article.

- *Workshops* – Attend local library and technology workshops.

- *Personnel development day* – A great idea to let each staff member have a day of learning.

- *Teleconferences* – Find out what sites host teleconferences in your area.

- *Webinars or Webcasts* – View a live or archived technology-related Webinar.

- *Work experience* – Try it out, join a team, volunteer for a project.

- *Work shadowing* – Observe other trainers at your library or other libraries.

- *Read and comment on blogs* – Join lists to dialogue on training and technology topics.

## Resources for Training Materials

Libraries love to share! Visit these Web sites to borrow handouts and PowerPoint slides and get ideas for workshops:

- *Akron-Summit County (OH) Public Library*
  (ascpl.lib.oh.us/training/handouts.html) – Very thorough
  handouts for library workshops on everything from
  Introduction to Computers to eBay and Blogging.

- *Hennepin County Library's Extranet*
  (www.hclib.org/extranet) – Includes trainer outlines,
  PowerPoint presentations, and handouts for workshops
  for the public.

- *InfoPeople* (www.infopeople.org) – Archived Webcasts,
  podcasts, and training materials such as handouts and
  PowerPoints, as well as resources for training. InfoPeople
  is a statewide LSTA project that functions as the training
  arm of the California State Library.

- *MERLOT: Multimedia Educational Resource for Learning
  and Online Teaching* (merlot.org) – Created by California
  State University in 1997 and free to all users, MERLOT is
  supported by a variety of schools, systems, and organizations. Individual membership also is free, and any member can submit a learning object to MERLOT. Materials
  are submitted by faculty members who are experts in
  their content areas, and a peer-review system is in place
  to make sure that the materials are of high quality.

- *Milwaukee Public Library* (www.mpl.org/file/computer_
  curriculums.htm) – Outlines and handouts on various
  popular workshops.

- *Oregon Library Instruction Wiki* (instructionwiki.org) –
  Oregon Library Association's Library Instruction
  Roundtable's collaboratively developed resource for
  librarians involved with or interested in instruction.
  Includes handouts, tutorials, and teaching techniques.

- *PRIMO: Peer-Reviewed Instructional Materials Online
  Database* (www.ala.org/CFApps/Primo/public/
  search.cfm) – PRIMO is hosted by ALA's Association of

College and Research Libraries to share peer-reviewed instructional materials created by librarians to teach people about discovering, accessing, and evaluating information in networked environments. Currently includes more than 145 projects.

- *TechAtlas* (techatlas.org) – Free online technology assessment and inventory tool, including staff skills surveys.

- *WebJunction* (webjunction.org)

  - Materials for Working with Computers and Spanish Speakers (webjunction.org/do/Navigation?category=7843)

  - Internet Resources for Patrons (webjunction.org/do/Navigation?category=518)

  - Training Materials (webjunction.org/do/Navigation?category=543)

  - Creating lesson plans for teaching the public (web junction.org/do/DisplayContent?id=1243) – Article by the Hibbing Public Library, includes links to lesson plans

## Online Tutorials

There are many online tutorials that you can access for free, and even incorporate into your workshops:

- *Akron-Summit County (OH) Public Library* (ascpl.lib.oh.us/training/tutorials.html) – A variety of tutorials.

- *Chris Rippel's Mouserobics* (www.ckls.org/~crippel/computerlab/tutorials/mouse/page1.html) – A popular tutorial for using the mouse. Rippel works at the Central Kansas Library System, Great Bend, Kansas.

- *Free Online Library Tutorials* (stephaniegerding.com/ tutorials) – A collection of various free library-related online tutorials maintained by the author.

- *Learn the Net* (www.learnthenet.com) – Interactive and animated tutorials on Internet basics.

- *LibraryU* (learning.libraryu.org) – LibraryU in Illinois has free self-paced tutorials on a variety of library topics such as administration, basic technology, marketing, and developing Web-based instruction.

- *University of North Texas Lifelong Education @ Desktop* (web2.unt.edu/cmp_lead) – Many tutorials are available, all specifically written for libraries. Fee-based, but can be purchased as a package for multiple users at a very affordable rate.

## Training and Technology-Related Web Sites

These Web sites offer helpful resources for trainers:

- *Bob Pike Group* (www.bobpikegroup.com) – Books, seminars, and creative training techniques workshops.

- *Center for Accelerated Learning* (www.alcenter.com/ alindex.html) – Includes tips, information about the Accelerated Learning Training Methods workshops, and *The Accelerated Learning Handbook* by Dave Meier.

- *Guide on the Side Columns by Marie Wallace* (www.llrx. com/cgi-bin/llrx.cgi?function=browseauth2&id=9) – Training-related issues.

- *Kipp Brothers* (www.kipptoys.com) – Source for buying cheap training incentives (toys).

- *Oriental Trading Company* (www.orientaltrading.com) – A great source for buying cheap training incentives (toys).

- *Pew Internet and American Life Project* (www.pew internet.org) – Reports and statistics on how Americans are using the Internet.

- *SnagIt* (www.techsmith.com) – Great screen-capturing program.

- *TechSoup's Community Technology Centers Section* (www.techsoup.org/learningcenter/ctc) – Community technology centers (CTCs) face many of the same issues that other public access computing centers face. This section of TechSoup contains articles that will help you build your library into a thriving learning center.

- *Teaching Tips Index*, Honolulu Community College Intranet (honolulu.hawaii.edu/intranet/committees/ FacDevCom/guidebk/teachtip/teachtip.htm) – Tons of great information.

- *TechSoup's Training Section* (www.techsoup.org/learning center/training) – Includes training articles on a variety of topics.

- *The Masie Center Learning LAB and ThinkTank* (www.masieweb.com) – An international think tank focused on the changing workforce and how people learn and perform.

- *Tools for E-Learning Trainers and Designers* (web junction.org/do/DisplayContent?id=14410) – Visit Dale Musselman's collection of links to rapid creation tools, live online training systems, and sites to share and borrow content.

- *Trainer's Warehouse* (www.trainerswarehouse.com) – Source for training supplies, manipulatives, and copyright free music.

- *Zoomerang* (zoomerang.com) – An easy-to-use online survey tool, with a free, lightweight version available.

## Webcasts and Webinars

Keep current and provide staff training by attending live or archived presentations broadcast on the Internet:

- *C|NET* (courses.help.com) – Free online courses on a variety of technology topics such as PowerPoint, PC Troubleshooting, and Digital Photography.

- *College of DuPage Press Library Teleconferences* (www.dupagepress.com/COD) – Programs can be viewed via satellite downlink, Webinar, or DVD. Some state libraries, library consortia, and cooperatives purchase subscriptions for entire states or regions.

- *Hewlett-Packard HP Online Courses* (hponline courses.com) – Free courses on topics such as digital photography, Excel, graphic design, and scanning basics.

- *Library of Congress Webcasts* (www.loc.gov/today/cyberlc) – Topics include History, Culture, Education, Government, Literature, Religion, Science, and Technology.

- *Medical Library Association Distance Education Program Resources* (www.mlanet.org/education) – Includes some technology topics.

- *OPAL: Online Programming for All Libraries* (www.opal-online.org) – OPAL is a collaborative effort by libraries of all types to provide free Web-based programs and training for library users and library staff members. You can find free courses such as the Ten Top Technologies for Librarians, Day of the Digital Audio Book, Wikis, and How to Google: An Introduction to Searching the Web.

- *SirsiDynix Institute* (www.sirsidynixinstitute.com) – Free Webinars, including archived training on Blogs & Libraries, Library 2.0, Gaming, and so on.

- *WebJunction's Online Courses* (webjunction.org/do/
  Navigation?category=442) – Everything from basic
  computing skills to training on advocacy and outreach.

- *WebJunction Webinars* (webjunction.org/do/
  Navigation?category=12365) – Live and archived free
  Webinars on topics including technology, training, and
  outreach.

## Library Technology-Related Blogs

The following Web sites are regularly updated with training
topics:

- *ALA TechSource Blog* (www.techsource.ala.org/blog) –
  Published by the American Library Association, with
  authors Michelle Boule, Michael Casey, Michael Golrick,
  Teresa Koltzenburg, Jenny Levine, Tom Peters, Karen G.
  Schneider, and Michael Stephens.

- *BlogJunction* (blog.webjunctionworks.org) –
  WebJunction's staff-authored blog will keep you up-to-
  date on events, programs, and staff observations.

- *Information Wants to Be Free* (meredith.wolfwater.com/
  wordpress/index.php) – Meredith Farkas, Distance
  Learning Librarian at Norwich University, includes posts
  on the library profession and technology.

- *It's All Good* (scanblog.blogspot.com) – Maintained by
  five OCLC staff members who post about "all things present and future that impact libraries and library users."

- *LibrarianInBlack* (librarianinblack.typepad.com/librari-
  aninblack) – By Sarah Houghton-Jan, Information and
  Web Services Manager for the San Mateo County Library,
  who writes "resources and discussions for the 'tech-
  librarians-by-default' among us."

- *Stephen's Lighthouse* (stephenslighthouse.sirsidynix.com) – By Stephen Abram, SirsiDynix's Vice President of Innovation, who includes his thoughts on library technology issues and notes from his national presentations.

- *Tame the Web: Libraries and Technology* (tametheweb.com) – Michael Stephens, instructor in the Graduate School of Library and Information Science at Dominican University, focuses on Web 2.0 and Library 2.0, technology-related articles and presentations, and technology trends.

- *The Shifted Librarian* (www.theshiftedlibrarian.com) – Jenny Levine, ALA Internet Development Specialist and Strategy Guide, posts on technology gadgets, gaming, and social technologies.

## Training Discussion Lists

Here are a few online discussion lists you can subscribe to via e-mail:

- *CLENERT* – The discussion list of ALA's Continuing Library Education and Networking Exchange Round Table (www.ala.org/ala/clenert/discussionlist/discussionlist.htm)

- *LEARNING-ORG* – The Learning Organization Mailing List (www.learning-org.com/LOinfo.html)

- *TRDEV* – The Training and Development Discussion Group (finance.groups.yahoo.com/group/trdev)

## Podcasts

These are audio only broadcasts that can be downloaded for free online:

- *CNET Networks* (CNET.com) – Includes podcasts such as Buzz Out Loud, Gadgettes, and MP3 Insider.

- *Talking with Talis* (talk.talis.com) – Listen to conversations about the interface between Web 2.0, libraries, and the Semantic Web.

- *TWiT: This Week in Tech* (www.twit.tv) – Free podcasts on technology topics.

## Professional Training Organizations

Membership in these organizations provides networking opportunities and tools such as training newsletters:

- *ASTD* (www.astd.org) – The American Society for Training & Development (ASTD) is a professional association dedicated to workplace learning and performance professionals. It began in 1944 and provides certification.

- *CLENE* (www.ala.org/ala/clenert) – The American Library Association (ALA) sponsors a Continuing Library Education Network and Exchange (CLENE) Round Table. Its goal is to promote quality continuing education for all library personnel. Membership includes membership to the American Management Association.

- *Library Instruction Round Table* (www3.baylor.edu/LIRT) – LIRT is a roundtable of the American Library Association and advocates library instruction as a means for developing competent library and information use as a part of lifelong learning. Many members are academic librarians.

## Training Scholarships

Apply for a training scholarship to attend a course or conference:

- *American Library Association* (www.ala.org) – Look under "awards, grants and scholarships." Also, look under divisions such as ACRL, AASL, LITA, PLA.

- *Special Library Association* (www.sla.org/content/learn/ scholarship/index.cfm) – See if your state chapter offers professional development awards.

- *Your State Library* (www.publiclibraries.com/state_ library.htm)

- *Your State Library Association and Regional Association* (www.ala.org/ala/ourassociation/chapters/stateand regional/stateregional.htm)

## Recommended Reading: Books

These books provide additional training information:

- American Society for Training and Development (ASTD). *INFO-LINE Series.* Alexandria. VA: ASTD – ASTD publishes a series of booklets on a variety of topics central to training design and delivery. The booklets offer concise "how-to" information.

- Jean Barbazette. *The Trainer's Support Handbook: A Practical Guide to Managing the Administrative Details of Training.* McGraw-Hill, 2001 – Includes downloadable handouts.

- Elaine Biech. *Training for Dummies.* Indianapolis, Indiana: Wiley Publishing, 2005.

- Sharon Bowman. *The Ten-Minute Trainer: 150 Ways to Teach It Quick and Make it Stick!* San Francisco: John Wiley & Sons, 2005.

- C. Leslie Charles, and Chris Clarke-Epstein. *The Instant Trainer: Quick Tips on How to Teach Others What You Know.* New York: McGraw-Hill, 1998.

- Paul Clothier. *The Complete Computer Trainer.* New York: McGraw Hill, 1996 – Wonderful resource, though not focused on library issues. This book still remains my top pick for new technology trainers.

- Robert Jolles. *How to Run Seminars and Workshops.* John Wiley & Sons, 2000 – Focuses on involving adult learners, using training technologies, planning, and more.

- Dave Meier. *The Accelerated Learning Handbook.* New York: McGraw Hill, 2000 – Learn to tap into the minds and personalities of all learning styles and enhance retention.

- Robert Pike. *Creative Training Techniques Handbook: Tips, Tactics, & How-Tos for Delivering Effective Training* (3rd edition). Amherst, MA: HRD Press, 2003 – I'd recommend all of Pike's many books.

- Mel Silberman. *Active Training: A Handbook of Techniques, Designs, Case Examples, and Tips.* San Francisco: Jossey-Bass, Pfeiffer, 1998.

- Harold Stolovitch and Erica Keeps. *Telling Ain't Training.* Alexandria, VA: American Society for Training & Development, 2002.

## Recommended Reading: Magazines/Journals

The following print resources can help you keep up-to-date on technology and training issues:

- ALA's *Smart Libraries* newsletter (www.techsource.ala.org/sln), *TechSource Online* (www.techsource.ala.org/ala-techsource-online.html), and *Library Technology Reports* (www.techsource.ala. org/ltr)

- *Computers in Libraries* (www.infotoday.com/cilmag)

- *PC Magazine* (www.pcmag.com)

- *PC World* (www.pcworld.com)

- *Searcher* (www.infotoday.com/searcher)

- *Smart Computing* (www.smartcomputing.com)

- *Technology Reviews* (www.technologyreview.com)

- *Training & Development Journal* (www.astd.org/astd/publications/td_magazine)

## Additional Tips from the Experts

**Survey question: What helpful training and technology-related resources (books, Web sites, blogs, etc.) do you use on a regular basis?**

*Michael Porter, Community Associate, WebJunction, Seattle (WA) –* "It depends on what subjects I am teaching. I try to stay over-informed on a few things so I can always throw in a few very recent news bits/examples so people know I'm on top of things. I read a lot of blogs. I teach tech stuff a lot, so I read *Wired* front to back every issue. I also read *Business 2.0* and pick up gadget magazines as well."

*Chris Peters, Information Technology Specialist, Washington State Library, Olympia (WA) –* "Del.icio.us is now my starting point for tech-related searches. I can see immediately how many del.icio.us users have bookmarked a site, and popular sites are usually useful and accurate. With search engines on the other hand, the top-ranked sites are often popular due to good search engine optimization on the part of the designer. I use Wikipedia a lot also."

*Anonymous* – "The *Dummies* series for Microsoft applications."

*Erin James, Library Associate, Gwinnett County Public Library, Lilburn (GA)* – "I read Lifehacker.com daily—it covers a lot more than I'd ever get to do in-branch, but I feel informed and more confident. I couldn't get by without Google—I can put in something as meaningless as an error code and get answers in seconds."

# Expert Library Technology Trainers

The following library technology trainers provided valuable training tips, insights, and advice, and their input has been used throughout. They are listed in order alphabetically by last name.

Max Anderson, Educational Services Librarian, SOLINET, Atlanta (GA)

Helene Blowers, Technology Director, Public Library of Charlotte & Mecklenburg County, Charlotte (NC)

Colleen Eggett, Training Coordinator, Utah State Library, Salt Lake City (UT)

Meredith Farkas, Distance Learning Librarian, Norwich University, Northfield (VT)

Scott Hines, Reference Librarian, Pacific Graduate School of Psychology, Palo Alto (CA)

Brenda Hough, Technology Coordinator, Northeast Kansas Library System, Lawrence (KS)

Sarah Houghton-Jan, Information and Web Services Manager, San Mateo County Library, San Mateo (CA)

Erin James, Library Associate, Gwinnett County Public Library, Lilburn (GA)

Mindy Johnson, Head of Adult Services, Camden County Library, Voorhees (NJ)

Chris Peters, Information Technology Specialist, Washington State Library, Olympia (WA)

Jana Ponce-Wolfe, Director, Parker Public Library, Parker (AZ)

Michael Porter, Community Associate, WebJunction, Seattle
(WA)

Bernadette Rivard, Supervisor of Technical Services, Milford
Town Library, Milford (MA)

Mary Bucher Ross, training consultant, former manager of Staff
Develoment, Seattle Public Library, Seattle (WA)

Michael Stephens, Instructor, Graduate School of Library &
Information Science at Dominican University, River Forrest
(IL)

Susannah Violino, Reference Librarian, Norwalk Public Library,
Norwalk (CT)

# *The Accidental Technology Trainer* Survey Questions

This survey was posted as an online form from January to March 2007 (home.earthlink.net/~stephaniegerding/accidentaltechnology trainer). Announcements were posted on appropriate e-mail lists and blogs, and also sent to specific individuals. Respondents are self-described library technology trainers. This is not a scientific survey, and no attempt was made to qualify respondents prior to their answering these questions.

## The Accidental Technology Trainer

Survey responses may be used in the forthcoming book, *The Accidental Technology Trainer,* to be published by Information Today, Inc. To complete this survey, you don't need to answer every question, but please answer as many as possible.

Would you like to remain anonymous or may comments used in the book be attributed to you?

Name:

E-mail Address:

Employer:

Job Title:

City and State:

How did you become a library technology trainer?

Explain how you use any of the more "traditional" library skills in providing training.

What types of technology workshops are offered by your library?

Which classes are the most popular/HOT? Provide descriptions if available.

How do you publicize your workshops? Please e-mail me examples of flyers, etc., to be shared.

How are your workshops funded? Explain funds/equipment derived from fundraising or sponsorships.

How do you handle waiting lists for classes? Are you able to offer enough workshops?

Do you provide workshops for the business community, Spanish-speakers, or other specialized target audiences? If so, please list all audiences, how you determine their needs, and adapt marketing to them.

How do you use community partners or other local resources in your workshops?

Give an example of a particularly difficult training experience and how you resolved the issue.

Share a favorite technology analogy that you use.

Describe your best training idea or advice to share with accidental technology trainers.

List helpful training and technology-related resources (books, Web sites, blogs, etc.) you use on a regular basis.

# Training Materials and Sample Workshop Flyers

Here you will find a few helpful training materials for you to use. The first two items include a checklist for self-assessment of your training skills and a template to use when writing workshop plans. The rest of the materials include sample technology training schedules and flyers used by exemplary libraries:

1. Accidental Library Technology Trainer Self-Assessment Checklist (pages 212–213)

2. Workshop Plan Template (page 214)

3. Barton County Library, Computer Training Schedule, Lamar, MO (page 215)

4. Morrill Public Library, Center for Lifelong Learning Class Schedule, Hiawatha, KS (pages 216–217)

5. Princeton Public Library, Databytes flyer, Princeton, NJ (page 218)

6. Princeton Public Library, Fun with Flickr flyer, Princeton, NJ (page 219)

7. Princeton Public Library, Tech Talks flyer, Princeton, NJ (page 220)

8. Martin County Library Systems, Computer Classes Schedule, Martin County, FL (pages 221–222)

9. Milford Town Library, Pre-Registration Survey, Milford, MA (page 223)

10. Akron-Summit County Public Library, Computer Training Schedule, Akron, OH (page 224)

### Accidental Library Technology Trainer Self-Assessment Checklist

Use this checklist to identify any of your skills or abilities that need improvement:

- ☐ Activity design: participant centered
- ☐ Activity design: small group
- ☐ Assessing individual learning needs
- ☐ Audiovisual use
- ☐ Body language
- ☐ Checking for understanding
- ☐ Coaching
- ☐ Communicating effectively
- ☐ Creativity
- ☐ Credibility
- ☐ Delivery techniques
- ☐ Empathy
- ☐ Encouraging independence
- ☐ Encouraging participation
- ☐ Environment—Optimal learning
- ☐ Evaluation techniques
- ☐ Facilitation
- ☐ Flexibility
- ☐ Follow-up
- ☐ Friendly
- ☐ Fun
- ☐ Group dynamics
- ☐ Inspiring
- ☐ Learning objectives
- ☐ Learning principles
- ☐ Learning styles
- ☐ Listening
- ☐ Managing difficult situations

- ☐ Managing timing/pace
- ☐ Organizational skills
- ☐ Outcomes
- ☐ Participant encouragement
- ☐ Patience
- ☐ People-oriented
- ☐ Practices
- ☐ Presentation skills
- ☐ Problem-solver
- ☐ Project management skills
- ☐ Providing feedback to participants
- ☐ Questioning skills
- ☐ Rapport building
- ☐ Reading learners
- ☐ Reinforcing participant's success
- ☐ Relevant
- ☐ Respect
- ☐ Sharing personal examples
- ☐ Speaking clearly and projecting
- ☐ Staying focused
- ☐ Stimulating learner motivation
- ☐ Strong introductions
- ☐ Visuals
- ☐ Workshop planning skills

Ongoing:
- ☐ Become experts and contribute to the field by writing articles and books
- ☐ Constantly update and improve content based on organizational and participant needs
- ☐ Continuous learning, updating skills and knowledge
- ☐ Incorporates feedback
- ☐ Life-long learners

## Workshop Plan Template

**Title**:

**Target Audience**:

**Length**:

**Workshop Goal:**

**Learning Objectives**:


**Description**:


**Modules and Timing**:

| Time | Module | Description |
|------|--------|-------------|
|      |        |             |
|      |        |             |
|      |        |             |
|      |        |             |
|      |        |             |
|      |        |             |
| Total: |      |             |

**Evaluation Process**:


**Handouts, Materials and Supplies**:

C-5

**Barton County Library**
**Computer Training Schedule**
**For Jan-Feb-March 2007**

**All classes are FREE!**
**Registration is limited. Please call 417/682-5355 to register.**

| Senior Citizen | Beginner | Basic | Intermediate | Advanced |
|---|---|---|---|---|
| New computer user Slower paced class | New computer user | Intro to Basic skills | Building on basic skills | Complex skills |

| Date/Time | Class | Class Description |
|---|---|---|
| 01/23/07 1:00–3:00 (T) | New Camera—Intro to Digital cameras BRING YOUR CAMERA IF YOU HAVE ONE! | Learn about taking pictures with a digital camera. Topics include: how to choose a digital camera, getting the most out of the features of your camera, and tips for taking good digital pictures. Lecture style class, not a "how-to". |
| 01/23/07 6:30-8:30 (T) | New Camera—Intro to Digital cameras BRING YOUR CAMERA IF YOU HAVE ONE! | Learn about taking pictures with a digital camera. Topics include: how to choose a digital camera, getting the most out of the features of your camera, and tips for taking good digital pictures. Lecture style class, not a "how-to". |
| 01/24/07 1:00–3:00 (W) | Working with Digital Pictures BRING YOUR PROBLEM PICTURES! | Learn how to get the most out of your digital pictures. Topics include: editing, sizing, cropping, and storing digital pictures using available free or inexpensive software. Hands-on exercises. |
| 01/24/07 6:30-8:30 (W) | Working with Digital Pictures BRING YOUR PROBLEM PICTURES! | Learn how to get the most out of your digital pictures. Topics include: editing, sizing, cropping, and storing digital pictures using available free or inexpensive software. Hands-on exercises. |
| 01/25/07 6:30-8:30 (Th) | Advanced Picture Editing with—MS Digital Pro Should have experience in editing of digital photos | Learn how to edit your digital pictures using one of the top photo editing software products available. Hands-on exercises. |
| 02/27/06 1:00–3:00 (T) | I don't do Windows! For beginners! | Learn the basics of using a computer: terminology; using Windows; working with files, and getting help. Lecture style class with some hands-on practice. |
| 02/28/07 1:00–3:00 (T) | Intro to Microsoft Word Should have basic mouse and windows skills | Learn the tools and features of Word. Topics include: cut and paste, move, and using templates. Students will create a report and a press release. |
| 02/28/07 6:30-8:30 (W) | Intro to Microsoft Word Should have basic mouse and windows skills | Learn the tools and features of Word. Topics include: cut and paste, move, and using templates. Students will create a report and a press release. |
| 03/01/07 1:00  3:00 (Th) | Advanced MS Word (formatting) Should have basic MS Word skills | Learn how to format a document using MS Word margins, tabs, and line spacing Hands-on exercises. |
| 03/01/07 6:30–8:30 (Th) | Advanced MS Word (formatting) Should have basic MS Word skills | Learn how to format a document using MS Word margins, tabs, and line spacing Hands-on exercises. |
| 03/027/07 1:00–3:00 (T) | Intro to Internet Should have basic mouse and Windows skills | Learn how to search the web easily and effectively. Topics include: browsers, search engines, world wide web, URL addresses, browsing web pages, page navigation, hyperlinks, favorites downloading files, printing, security, and lots of hands-on surfing. |
| 03/27/07 6:30-8:30 (T) | Intro to Internet Should have basic mouse and Windows skills | Learn how to search the web easily and effectively. Topics include: browsers, search engines, world wide web, URL addresses, browsing web pages, page navigation, hyperlinks, favorites downloading files, printing, security, and lots of hands-on surfing. |
|  | Internet Research CANCELLED | For advanced users of the Internet. Search tips on how to limit the number of responses to your search by using a Boolean search, specialty search engines, and how to evaluate web sites. Lots of hands-on surfing. |
|  | Internet Research CANCELLED | For advanced users of the Internet. Search tips on how to limit the number of responses to your search by using a Boolean search, specialty search engines, and how to evaluate web sites. Lots of hands-on surfing. |
|  | Open Lab CANCELLED | Lab will be open for users of all skill areas. Help will be available as needed. Come and practice your computer skills, search the web, or play solitaire. |

### Class Schedule by Month

April
April 4    Wed    9:30am    Beginning Computer
April 4    Wed    11:00am   Beginning Computer
April 13   Fri    9:00am    Beginning Internet
April 13   Fri    11:00am   Beginning Internet
April 20   Fri    9:00am    Intro to Word
April 20   Fri    10:30am   Cut, Copy and Paste
April 23   Mon    6:00pm    Buying on eBay
April 25   Wed    10:00am   Yahoo or Hotmail
April 30   Mon    6:00pm    Selling on eBay

May
May 2      Wed    10:00am   Instant Messaging
May 11     Fri    9 - 12am  Drop In Computer Lab
May 18     Fri    10:00am   Glaciers of Mexico
May 21     Mon    5:30pm    Audio Books/Music

June
June 6     Wed    9:30am    Beginning Computer
June 6     Wed    11:00 am  Beginning Computer
June 15    Fri    9:00am    Word
June 15    Fri    10:30am   Cut, Copy and Paste
June 18    Mon    5:30 pm   Beginning Computer
June 22    Fri    10:00am   GPS for Kids
June 25    Mon    10:00am   Beginning Internet
June 25    Mon    6:00pm    Beginning Internet

Center for Lifelong Learning

## April
## May
## June
## 2007

Free Community
Education and
Computer Classes

---

**Two Easy Ways to Sign Up
for a Class**
Seating is limited for all classes except the
drop-in computer lab sessions so please
pre-register!

1. Call 785-742-3831
2. Stop by the Library

---

All classes are held in the
library meeting room (lower level).
Handicapped parking and access is
available at the south entrance.

---

**Earn Lifelong Learning Credits along the way!**
Earn "Lifelong Learning" credits for each class
you attend. Certificates will be awarded to those
achieving 10, 25, 50, 75 and 100 hours of credit.

---

Morrill Public Library
431 Oregon
Hiawatha, KS 66434
742-3831
www.hiawathalibrary.org

## Learn New Computer Skills

### Beginning Computing
April 4 Wednesday 9:30am and 11:00am
June 6 Wednesday 9:30am and 11:00am
June 18 Monday 5:30 pm
This is a very basic class for those new to a computer. Learn to hold and maneuver the mouse, type in a text box, use a scroll bar, and more. All other classes will be easier once you've mastered these skills. Come to a drop-in session to practice some more.

### Beginning Internet
April 13 Friday 9:00am and 11:00am
June 25 Monday 10:00am and 6:00pm
Learn basic surfing using Internet Explorer, and visit some interesting sites on the Web.

### Set up Yahoo or Hotmail E-Mail Account
April 25   Wednesday  10:00am
Yahoo and Hotmail are a free online services available from any computer with Internet access. Learn to address, compose, receive, and reply to e-mail messages.

### Instant Messaging for Beginners
May 2 Wednesday  10:00am
Join Anne and Rosma for an introduction and hands-on practice instant messaging. IM is a way to send live text messages to your friends and family when they are online — no matter where they are in the world! Participants must have a valid Yahoo or Hotmail e-mail account to participate in this class (see April 25 above).

### Drop-In Computer Lab Session
May 11 Friday 9 - 12am
Practice new computer skills or get answers to basic PC questions. If we don't know, we'll look it up! Come and go anytime during the session.

## Learn Word Processing

### Introduction to Microsoft Word
Learn the essentials of Microsoft Word - one of the most common word processing program used for creating reports, resumes, and much more. Learn to set margins, change fonts, spell check, select text, copy and move text, and more.

### Cut, Copy, and Paste
Learn some shortcuts for editing and moving text. Learn to select, cut, and copy text, and then paste it into another document. Also learn to copy web addresses or links and paste them into the browser address bar or a document.
April 20 Friday 9:00am (Word - followed by )
April 20 Friday 10:30am (Cut, copy and paste)
   or
June 15 Friday 9:00am (Word - followed by )
June 15 Friday 10:30am (Cut, copy and paste)

## New Two-Session eBay Series!

### Buy cool stuff on eBay
April 23 Monday 6:00pm
Learn the basics of setting up an eBay buyer account, searching for items, bidding successfully, purchasing with PayPal, and learning more about the seller you're dealing with. Lots of practical tips from Wendell Ganstrom.

### Sell your extra stuff on eBay
April 30 Monday 6:00pm
This class is an introduction to setting up an eBay seller account, writing item descriptions, putting photos on your auctions, getting paid, shipping, and much more!

## Just for Fun

### The Mountain Glaciers of Mexico
May 18 Friday 10:00am
Mexico doesn't conjure images of mountains, much less glaciers. However, did you know that some of the highest mountains and glaciers in North America are in the tropics of Mexico? Steve Brown will lead this pictorial tour of Mexico's volcano giants and an exploration of their glaciers. Along the way participants will hear the fascinating role they played in helping the Spanish conquer the Aztecs.

### Free Audio Books & Music
May 21 Monday 5:30pm
Use Overdrive to browse and search hundreds of digital titles and download to your computer, transfer to a portable MP3 device, or burn onto a CD for your reading and listening pleasure anywhere, anytime. Bring your MP3 player for the class or use one of ours.  (This class requires a current Kansas Library Card. Get yours at the circulation desk free anytime.)

### GPS for Kids
June 22 Friday 10:00am
The Global Positioning System can help you find any point on earth and is lots of fun. What kids don't know is that it's also very educational and lays a good foundation for learning geography, geometry and calculus. This program with Steve Brown will teach middle school age kids how to use a GPS receiver. We'll also be learning to play a fun "treasure hunt" game with GPS called geocaching. GPS receivers will be provided, but bring your own if you have one.

### Conversational Spanish with Aida
Begin learning or brush up on your Spanish skills in these informal sessions with Aida Jara. This class is designed for adults - high school age and older. Call the Library for next class dates.

PRINCETON PUBLIC 🏠 LIBRARY PRESENTS

# databytes

Lunchtime Explorations of the Library's Databases
in the Technology Center, second floor

## A Tour of Recent Subscriptions

Jane Brown, manager of Reference and Adult Services, will demonstrate several new additions
to our databases, including ProQuest Obituaries, the African-American Biographical Database,
Consumer Health Complete and others to our already extensive collection of databases
available for use from home, office or in the library with your card.

*December 13*

## Wilson Science Full-Text Select

This new, all-full-text database contains a broad range of important science literature from a
variety of fields. Included is content from Applied Science & Technology Full Text, Biological &
Agricultural Index Plus and General Science Full Text, plus additional related science titles
indexed by other Wilson databases.

*January 10, 24*

## EBSCO Update

One of our most popular databases at the library, EBSCOhost provides comprehensive access to
information in a variety of fields from your home or office with a library card. EBSCO has
added new content, most notably in the areas of consumer health and business, expanded the
full-text in several other disciplines and made several significant improvements to their search
interface. This session will help you get more from EBSCOhost.

*February 14, 28*

# Wednesdays, 1 p.m.

princeton
🏠

TECHNOLOGY CENTER, SECOND FLOOR, SANDS LIBRARY BUILDING
65 WITHERSPOON ST.   609.924.9529   princetonlibrary.org

PRINCETON PUBLIC LIBRARY PRESENTS
Fun *with*
flickr
Two-week course covering the basics of the innovative and interactive online photo management site that is becoming the most popular photo sharing site on the web!
It's easy to use and fun to browse!
10 a.m.
Tuesdays, Nov. 7 & 14
princeton
TECHNOLOGY CENTER SECOND FLOOR, SANDS LIBRARY BUILDING
65 WITHERSPOON ST. 609.924.9529 princetonlibrary.org

PRINCETON  PUBLIC  📖  LIBRARY  PRESENTS

**TUESDAY TECHNOLOGY TALKS**

March - May

**Zuula**: A New Metasearch Engine...from NJ

Tim Hunt, president of Zuula, a new metasearch
engine based right here in Princeton, will
describe the history of Zuula and demonstrate
some of the various special features that have
been attracting attention and garnering praise.

**Tuesday, March 6, 7 p.m.**

**ZUULA**™

**Extending Firefox**

John LeMasney, of Rider University, will talk about the
best 25 free extensions and add-ons for the popular
Firefox web browser to deal with media, productivity,
information management, entertainment, and more.

**Tuesday, April 3, 7 p.m.**

**What's New & Cool?** PPL Tech Team & Open Mic Night

Get to know Princeton Public Library's technology
training team as they reveal all about their favorite
sites and recent discoveries. Then, it's your turn.
What sites do you use daily? What is really useful to you?

**Tuesday, May 1, 7 p.m.**

princeton  COMMUNITY ROOM, FIRST FLOOR, SANDS LIBRARY BUILDING
65 WITHERSPOON ST. 609.924.9529 princetonlibrary.org

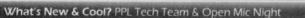

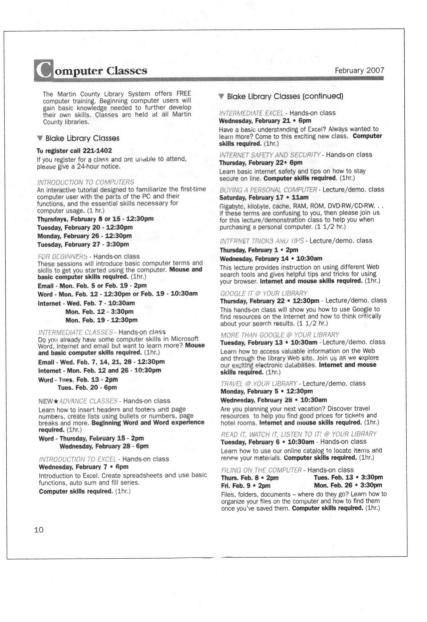

# Computer Classes

February 2007

The Martin County Library System offers FREE computer training. Beginning computer users will gain basic knowledge needed to further develop their own skills. Classes are held at all Martin County libraries.

### ▼ Blake Library Classes

**To register call 221-1402**
If you register for a class and are unable to attend, please give a 24-hour notice.

*INTRODUCTION TO COMPUTERS*
An interactive tutorial designed to familiarize the first-time computer user with the parts of the PC and their functions, and the essential skills necessary for computer usage. (1 hr.)
**Thursdays, February 8 or 15 - 12:30pm**
**Tuesday, February 20 - 12:30pm**
**Monday, February 26 - 12:30pm**
**Tuesday, February 27 - 3:30pm**

*FOR BEGINNERS* - Hands-on class
These sessions will introduce basic computer terms and skills to get you started using the computer. **Mouse and basic computer skills required.** (1hr.)
**Email - Mon. Feb. 5 or Feb. 19 - 2pm**
**Word - Mon. Feb. 12 - 12:30pm or Feb. 19 - 10:30am**
**                Mon. Feb. 12 - 3:30pm**
**Internet - Wed. Feb. 7 - 10:30am**
**                   Mon. Feb. 19 - 12:30pm**

*INTERMEDIATE CLASSES* - Hands-on class
Do you already have some computer skills in Microsoft Word, Internet and email but want to learn more? **Mouse and basic computer skills required.** (1hr.)
**Email - Wed. Feb. 7, 14, 21, 28 - 12:30pm**
**Internet - Mon. Feb. 12 and 26 - 10:30pm**
**Word - Tues. Feb. 13 - 2pm**
**            Tues. Feb. 20 - 6pm**

*NEW★ADVANCE CLASSES* - Hands-on class
Learn how to insert headers and footers and page numbers, create lists using bullets or numbers, page breaks and more. **Beginning Word and Word experience required.** (1hr.)
**Word - Thursday, February 15 - 2pm**
**            Wednesday, February 28 - 6pm**

*INTRODUCTION TO EXCEL* - Hands-on class
**Wednesday, February 7 • 6pm**
Introduction to Excel. Create spreadsheets and use basic functions, auto sum and fill series.
**Computer skills required.** (1hr.)

### ▼ Blake Library Classes (continued)

*INTERMEDIATE EXCEL* - Hands-on class
**Wednesday, February 21 • 6pm**
Have a basic understanding of Excel? Always wanted to learn more? Come to this exciting new class. **Computer skills required.** (1hr.)

*INTERNET SAFETY AND SECURITY* - Hands-on class
**Thursday, February 22• 6pm**
Learn basic internet safety and tips on how to stay secure on line. **Computer skills required.** (1hr.)

*BUYING A PERSONAL COMPUTER* - Lecture/demo. class
**Saturday, February 17 • 11am**
Gigabyte, kilobyte, cache, RAM, ROM, DVD-RW/CD-RW. . . if these terms are confusing to you, then please join us for this lecture/demonstration class to help you when purchasing a personal computer. (1 1/2 hr.)

*INTERNET TRICKS AND TIPS* - Lecture/demo. class
**Thursday, February 1 • 2pm**
**Wednesday, February 14 • 10:30am**
This lecture provides instruction on using different Web search tools and gives helpful tips and tricks for using your browser. **Internet and mouse skills required.** (1hr.)

*GOOGLE IT @ YOUR LIBRARY*
**Thursday, February 22 • 12:30pm** - Lecture/demo. class
This hands-on class will show you how to use Google to find resources on the Internet and how to think critically about your search results. (1 1/2 hr.)

*MORE THAN GOOGLE @ YOUR LIBRARY*
**Tuesday, February 13 • 10:30am** - Lecture/demo. class
Learn how to access valuable information on the Web and through the library Web site. Join us as we explore our exciting electronic databases. **Internet and mouse skills required.** (1hr.)

*TRAVEL @ YOUR LIBRARY* - Lecture/demo. class
**Monday, February 5 • 12:30pm**
**Wednesday, February 28 • 10:30am**
Are you planning your next vacation? Discover travel resources to help you find good prices for tickets and hotel rooms. **Internet and mouse skills required.** (1hr.)

*READ IT, WATCH IT, LISTEN TO IT! @ YOUR LIBRARY*
**Tuesday, February 6 • 10:30am** - Hands-on class
Learn how to use our online catalog to locate items and renew your materials. **Computer skills required.** (1hr.)

*FILING ON THE COMPUTER* - Hands-on class
**Thurs. Feb. 8 • 2pm              Tues. Feb. 13 • 3:30pm**
**Fri. Feb. 9 • 2pm                 Mon. Feb. 26 • 3:30pm**
Files, folders, documents – where do they go? Learn how to organize your files on the computer and how to find them once you've saved them. **Computer skills required.** (1hr.)

10

▼ Blake Library Classes (continued)

*ASK THE LINDAS* - Lecture/demo. class
**Tuesday, February 6 • 12:30pm**
Do you have a problem with the Internet, email or
Microsoft Word that you cannot solve? Library staff
computer instructors Linda Rech and Linda Sheldon will be
available to answer your computer-related questions. (1hr.)
Registration not required.

*BUYING A DIGITAL CAMERA* - Lecture/demo. class
**Thursday, February 8 • 6:30pm**
Megapixels, optical zoom, LCD screens, movie mode,
USB transfers – my goodness, this is confusing! Join us
to become familiar with the terminology to help you buy
a digital camera. **Computer skills required.** (1 1/2hr.)

*PHOTO EDITING* - Lecture/demo. class
**Thursday, February 15 • 6:30pm**
Discover the fundamentals of editing your digital
photographs. **Computer skills required.** (1 1/2hr.)

NEW★*BASIC COMPUTER MAINTENANCE* - Lecture/dem.
**Tuesday, February 6 • 2pm**    Learn a few simple tasks
to keep your computer running smoothly.  (1 hr.)

NEW★*HEALTH & WELLNESS* - Lecture/demo. class
**Tuesday, February 20 • 10:30am**
Learn how to access reliable sources for health
information. (1 hr.)

NEW★*WHAT ARE THEY TALKING ABOUT?* - Lecture/demo.
**Tuesday, February 27 • 2pm**
You Too? YouTube? If YouTube, MySpace, Wii, and iPod
are terms you've heard but don't understand, come to
this lecture/demo for an explanation. (1 hr.)

NEW★*E-CARDS* - Lecture/demo. class
**Tuesday, February 6 • 3:30pm**
**Tuesday, February 13 • 12:30pm**
Learn to personalize and send free holiday email cards
to family and friends. **Previous Internet experience
required.** (1 hr.)

▼ Hobe Sound Public Library Classes

*INDIVIDUAL HELP SESSIONS*
If you are using Word, email, Internet or Excel and are
having a problem, you may schedule an appointment for
an individual session by calling Linda Sheldon,
221-1402.

*COMPUTER WORKSHOP* - Lecture/demo. class
Walk-ins welcome. **Registration not required.** This is an
after library hours class.
**1st and 2nd Thursday of the month • 7pm - 9pm**
New or experienced computer users are invited to bring
their computer questions to this session. A wide range
of topics from beginner to advanced will be included.

▼ Hoke Library Classes

See the Hoke Library page (page 7) for a listing of
computer classes at the Hoke Library in Jensen Beach.

▼ Cummings Library Classes

**To register call 221-1402**
*INTRODUCTION TO COMPUTERS*
**Wednesday, February 28 • 10am** - Hands-on class
An interactive tutorial designed to familiarize the first-
time computer user with the parts of the PC and their
functions, and the essential skills necessary for computer usage.

▼ Elisabeth Lahti Library Classes

**To register call 597-4200**
*COMPUTER 101* - Hands-on class
**2nd Wednesday • 11am**
A basic class geared for the beginner.  Topics include
an introduction to the Windows environment and practice tutorials using the keyboard and mouse. (1hr.)

*INTERNET I* - Hands-on class
**1st Saturday • 9am**
Get connected to the Internet! Learn how to use the
Internet and how to open Web sites using a browser.
(1hr.) **Prerequisite: Computer 101**

*INTERNET I (SPANISH)* - Hands-on class
**2nd Saturday • 9am**
Get connected to the Internet! Learn how to use the
Internet and how to open Web sites using a browser.
(1hr.) **Prerequisite: Computer 101**

*EMAIL I* - Hands-on class
**3rd Saturday • 9am**
Sign up for a free email account. Learn to open a Web
site and fill out an online registration form to sign up
for an email address. (1hr.) **Prerequisite: Computer 101**

NEW★*PHOTO EDITING* - Lecture/demo. class
**Wednesday, February 7 • 11am**
Discover the fundamentals of editing your digital
photographs. **Computer skills required.** (1 1/2hr.)

▼ Robert Morgade Library Classes

**To register call 221-1402**
*INDIVIDUAL HELP SESSIONS*
If you are using Word, email, Internet or Excel and are
having a problem, you may schedule an appointment for
an individual session by calling Linda Sheldon, 221-1402.

*MICROSOFT WORD* - Hands-on class
**Monday, February 5 • 9am**
Introduction to Word. Learn to create and save docu-
ments. **Computer skills required.** (1hr.)

11

# Computer Training at the MTL

*Pre-Registration*

*Survey*

Please complete the following survey so that we may plan the computer training sessions to best meet the needs of our patrons.

We will contact you with the dates for training that will best match your skill level.

**Return to:**
Bernadette Rivard
Supervisor of Technical Services
Milford Town Library
80 Spruce Street
Milford, MA 01757

1. Have you ever taken a typing/keyboarding class?
   _____ Yes
   _____ No
   _____ No, but I have good typing skills

2. When did you last use a computer?
   _____ I have never used a computer
   _____ I have used a computer in the last year
   _____ I have used a computer in the last month
   _____ I have used a computer in the last week

3. How comfortable are you using a computer mouse?
   _____ I have never used a mouse
   _____ I have used a mouse but with great difficulty
   _____ I have used a mouse with some difficulty
   _____ I have used a mouse with no difficulty

4. Which of these computer functions have you used comfortably?
   _____ The Internet
   _____ E-Mail
   _____ Microsoft Word
   _____ Microsoft Excel, PowerPoint, Access or Publisher
   _____ Other, please specify _____

5. Do you have an e-mail address?
   _____ Yes and I check it regularly, the address is:
   _____ @ _____ . _____
   _____ Yes, but I do not check it regularly
   _____ No, and I am not interested in an e-mail account
   _____ No, but interested in setting up
            an e-mail account

I would prefer to attend sessions:
   _____ Weekday mornings, 10:00 am
   _____ Weekday evenings, 6:00 pm

   _____ Saturday morning, 10:00 am
   _____ Saturday afternoon, 2:30 pm
(Saturday classes school year only, classes limited)

I am interested in:

Information Literacy Series

   _____ * Using the Online Catalog
   _____ * Finding & Evaluating Information on the Internet
   _____ Researching Medical Conditions & Prescription Drugs
   _____ Researching Jobs, Careers & Companies
   _____ Researching Purchasing a Consumer Product

* These two classes are required before enrolling in any of the Research Classes.

Microsoft Office Series

   _____ * Word          _____ **Excel

   _____ PowerPoint      _____ Access

   _____ Publisher

* This class is required before enrolling in any other Microsoft Office class.

** This class is required before enrolling in Access

Name: _____

Address: _____

_____

City, State, Zip: _____

Telephone: _____

I am over 16 years of age _____

*Due to the upcoming renovation of the library, class offerings may be limited or postponed, depending upon space available.*

# Appendix D

# Web Sites

## Chapter 1

*Time*'s Person of the Year: YOU, www.time.com/time/magazine/
article/0,9171,1569514,00.html

Pew Internet & American Life Project, www.pewinternet.org

ALA Toward a National Library Agenda, wikis.ala.org/national
libraryagenda/images/f/f4/Discussion_Draft_MW_2007_final_
1-11-07.pdf

The Computer Moves In, www.time.com/time/printout/0,8816,
953632,00.html

Confronting the Challenges of Participatory Culture: Media
Education for the 21st Century, www.digitallearning.macfound.
org/site/c.enJLKQNlFiG/b.2029291/k.97E5/Occasional_Papers.
htm

## Chapter 2

Anytime, Anywhere Answers: Building Skills for Virtual Reference,
vrstrain.spl.org/vrstrainer.htm

## Chapter 3

Just-In-Time Teaching, serc.carleton.edu/sp/compadre/justin
time/index.html

## Chapter 4

The ABC's of Engineering Education, www.ncsu.edu/felder-public/Papers/ASEE04(ABCs).pdf

Index of Learning Styles (ILS), www.ncsu.edu/felder-public/ILSpage.html

## Chapter 5

Pfeiffer Home—Essential Resources for Training and HR Professionals, www.pfeiffer.com

## Chapter 7

Minnesota Voluntary Certification for Library Employees, www.arrowhead.lib.mn.us/certification/transfer.htm

California Library Association—Technology Core Competencies for California Library Workers, www.cla-net.org/included/docs/tech_core_competencies.pdf

Western Council of State Libraries/Continuum of Library Education Library Practitioner Core Competencies, westernco.org/continuum/LCPPfinal.pdf

Zoomerang, zoomerang.com

Survey Monkey, surveymonkey.com

PLA Service Responses draft, www.plaresults.org/service_response_links.htm

Volunteer Match, www.volunteermatch.org

Tempe Library Volunteer Opportunities for Students, www.tempe.gov/volunteer/libraryyouth.htm

San Mateo County Library—Internet Instruction image, www.smcl.org/libraries/mil/events/images/COMPUTER-CLASS. jpg

Milford Town Library Computer Workshops, www.milfordtown
library.org/computerworkshops.html
E•vanced Solutions home page, www.e-vancedsolutions.com

## Chapter 9

The Java Timer, html_help4u.tripod.com/javatime.html

## Chapter 10

The C's of our Sea Change, www.infotoday.com/cilmag/feb07/
Blowers_Reed.shtml
The Chicago Public Library Tech 37 Introduction, www.chipublib.
org/008subject/003cya/teened/tech37intro.html
Springfield-Greene County Library, thelibrary.springfield.
missouri.org
OpenOffice, openoffice.org
A Librarian Riding the Shift—Netguides, www.librarytechtonics.
info/archives/netguides
Five Weeks to a Social Library, www.sociallibraries.com/course

## Chapter 11

WebJunction—Materials for Working with Computers and Spanish
Speakers, webjunction.org/do/Navigation?category=7843
WebJunction—Internet Resources for Patrons, webjunction.org/
do/Navigation?category=518
WebJunction—Training Materials, webjunction.org/do/
Navigation? category=543
WebJunction—Creating Lesson Plans for Teaching the Public,
webjunction.org/do/DisplayContent?id=1243
TechAtlas, techatlas.org
InfoPeople, www.infopeople.org

Hennepin County Library's extranet, www.hclib.org/extranet

Oregon Library Instruction Wiki, instructionwiki.org

Peer-Reviewed Instructional Materials Online Database (Formerly Internet Education Project), www.ala.org/CFApps/Primo/public/search.cfm

Akron-Summit County Public Library Class Handouts, ascpl.lib.oh.us/training/handouts.html

Multimedia Educational Resource for Learning and Online Teaching, merlot.org

Milwaukee Public Library Computer Class Curriculums, www.mpl.org/file/computer_curriculums.htm

Central Kansas Library System—Welcome to Mouserobics! www.ckls.org/~crippel/computerlab/tutorials/mouse/page1.html

Akron-Summit County Public Library Computer Skills Tutorials, ascpl.lib.oh.us/training/tutorials.html

The Accidental Library Technology Trainer—Free Online Tutorials, stephaniegerding.com/tutorials

Learn the Net, www.learnthenet.com

The Center for Accelerated Learning, www.alcenter.com/al index.html

WebJunction—Tools for E-Learning Trainers and Designers, webjunction.org/do/DisplayContent?id=14410

TechSoup Learning Center—Training, www.techsoup.org/learningcenter/training

TechSoup Learning Center—Community Technology Center (CTC), www.techsoup.org/learningcenter/ctc

The MASIE Center Learning Lab and ThinkTank, www.masieweb.com

Law Library Resource Xchange, www.llrx.com/cgi-bin/llrx.cgi?function=browseauth2&id=9

Trainer's Warehouse, www.trainerswarehouse.com

Oriental Trading, www.orientaltrading.com

Kipp Brothers Toys, www.kipptoys.com

The Bob Pike Group, www.bobpikegroup.com

TechSmith Screen Capture Software, www.techsmith.com

Pew Internet & American Life Project, www.pewinternet.org

Honolulu Community College Faculty Development Teaching Tips, honolulu.hawaii.edu/intranet/committees/FacDevCom/ guidebk/teachtip/teachtip.htm

Zoomerang Online Survey Tool, Zoomerang.com

The Library of Congress Webcasts, www.loc.gov/today/cyberlc

Medical Library Association Education, www.mlanet.org/ education

WebJunction—Live Space Events, webjunction.org/do/Navi gation?category=12365

SirsiDynix Institute, www.sirsidynixinstitute.com

Online Programming for All Libraries, www.opal-online.org

WebJunction—Course Catalog, webjunction.org/do/Navigation? category=442

HP Online classes, hponlinecourses.com

CNET Online Courses, courses.help.com

ALA TechSource, www.techsource.ala.org/blog

Stephen's Lighthouse, stephenslighthouse.sirsidynix.com

Tame the Web: Libraries and Technology, tametheweb.com

BlogJunction, blog.webjunctionworks.org

It's All Good, scanblog.blogspot.com

LibrarianInBlack, librarianinblack.typepad.com/librarianin black

Information Wants to Be Free, meredith.wolfwater.com/word press/index.php

The Shifted Librarian, www.theshiftedlibrarian.com

ALA Continuing Library Education and Networking Exchange Round Table Discussion List, www.ala.org/ala/clenert/ discussionlist/discussionlist.htm

Learning Organization Mailing List and Archive, www.learning-org.com/LOinfo.html

The Training and Development Discussion Group, finance.groups.yahoo.com/group/trdev

TWiT: This Week in Tech, www.twit.tv

CNET Networks, CNET.com

Talking with Talis, talk.talis.com

The American Society for Training & Development, www. astd.org

ALA Continuing Library Education Network and Exchange Round Table, www.ala.org/ala/clenert

Library Instruction Round Table, www3.baylor.edu/LIRT

American Library Association, www.ala.org

Special Library Association Scholarships, www.sla.org/content/learn/scholarship/index.cfm

Your State Library, www.publiclibraries.com/state_library.htm

Your State Library Association and Regional Association, www.ala.org/ala/ourassociation/chapters/stateandregional/stateregional.htm

ALA's *Smart Libraries* newsletter, www.techsource.ala.org/sln

TechSource Online, www.techsource.ala.org/ala-techsource-online.html

*Library Technology Reports,* www.techsource.ala.org/ltr

*Computers in Libraries,* www.infotoday.com/cilmag

*PC Magazine,* www.pcmag.com

*PC World,* www.pcworld.com

*Searcher,* www.infotoday.com/searcher

*Smart Computing,* www.smartcomputing.com

*Technology Reviews,* www.technologyreview.com

*Training & Development Journal,* www.astd.org/astd/publications/td_magazine

# About the Author

**Stephanie Gerding**, an independent consultant, focuses her publications on training, technology, and fundraising for libraries, and loves to share her experiences by writing. Her first book, *Grants for Libraries*, was published in 2006 and received a starred review in *Library Journal*. She has written many articles for the library profession, including "Training Technology Trainers" for *Computers in Libraries*, and is the "Bringing in the Money" columnist for the Public Library Association's *Public Libraries* magazine. She has also been a newsletter editor for various library associations and is co-author of the Library Grants Blog (librarygrants. blogspot.com).

Having done a variety of training during her library career for all types of libraries—school, public, academic, and special— Stephanie has presented at national conferences and conducted training across the U.S., from Seattle to Florida, Maine to Hawaii, and many places in between. She has been involved in technology training throughout her library career and has trained librarians, systems administrators, homeless children, university students, teachers and healthcare workers in rural South Africa, and senior citizens.

She actually began her library career as an accidental library technology trainer. Her first experience conducting training was when she was asked to be the technical services department e-mail trainer in 1996 at an academic library, training staff on their very first e-mail system. She soon discovered she was adept at translating technology basics into an easy-to-understand format for others to learn. Her first professional position was with SIRSI, a library automation company. The company's philosophy at that time was that it would rather hire librarians to be trainers and teach them the technology, instead of hiring techies and teaching them the basics of librarianship so that they could understand their learners. Stephanie traveled around the country training staff in different library institutions, often on their first automation system.

Later, these skills became invaluable, as she trained thousands of librarians who found themselves accidental technology trainers. While working for the Bill & Melinda Gates Foundation's Library Program, she conducted hundreds of workshops, developed curricula, and produced materials for new library technology trainers who found themselves "accidentally" in charge of training staff and patrons when granted computers from the Gates Foundation. She traveled to libraries and also conducted weeklong train-the-trainer programs in Seattle. Many of these libraries were getting computers for the first time and were suddenly responsible for teaching other staff members as well as patrons.

Stephanie has also managed statewide library training programs at New Mexico and Arizona State libraries, including administration of four technology institutes, and customized on-site technology training programs for public libraries, managed a corporate library as a systems administrator, and taught Web-based distance education technology courses on information literacy and online learning for Northcentral University.

# Index

**M**